Skills
and
Applications
Handbook

Student Edition

author

Elizabeth A. Weaver

PEARSON

Boston, Massachusetts
Chandler, Arizona
Glenview, Illinois
Shoreview, Minnesota
Upper Saddle River, New Jersey

PEARSON

DRIVE RIGHT

ELEVENTH EDITION

Elizabeth A. Weaver is the Driver Education Specialist for the Idaho Department of Education.

Photographs
Every effort has been made to secure permission and provide appropriate credit for photographic material. The publisher deeply regrets any omission and pledges to correct errors called to its attention in subsequent editions.

Unless otherwise acknowledged, all photographs are the property of Pearson Education, Inc.

Photo locators denoted as follows: Top (T), Center (C), Bottom (B), Left (L), Right (R), Background (Bkgd)

Cover (T,C) Kimball Stock; (B) Shutterstock; (CC) Shutterstock. 50 (BL) dpa picture alliance/Alamy Stock Photo.

ISBN 0-13-361263-5
ISBN 978-0-13-361263-9

28   20

Contents

Name _____ Date _____

Pick a Word

Use the words in the box below to complete each statement.

collision	highway transportation system (HTS)	operating costs
driving task	IPDE Process	risk
fixed costs	low-risk driving	Zone Control System
graduated driver licensing program		

_____ 1. The _____ has three parts: people, vehicles, and roadways.

_____ 2. The main _____ of driving is the possibility of a conflict that leads to a collision.

_____ 3. As a driver, you are responsible for your _____ _____, which include the cost of fuel, oil, and tires.

_____ 4. The _____ includes all the social, physical, and mental skills required for low-risk driving.

_____ 5. A process of seeing, thinking, and responding is called the _____.

_____ 6. Your _____ are not determined by how many miles you drive and include the initial cost of your vehicle, licensing fees, and insurance.

_____ 7. A method for managing the space around your vehicle is called the _____.

_____ 8. _____ means driving in a way that reduces conflicts.

_____ 9. A(n) _____ is the product of human error.

_____ 10. A(n) _____ requires a young driver to go through a series of licensing stages.

Write the IPDE Step

_____ 1. You see a construction worker holding a warning sign.

_____ 2. You think the other driver does not see you.

_____ 3. You slow to increase your following distance.

_____ 4. You choose to flash your brake lights.

_____ 5. You need to change lanes.

_____ 6. You see a motorcyclist signaling for a left turn.

_____ 7. You change your lane position to increase space.

_____ 8. You think the vehicle's passenger door will open.

_____ 9. You notice gravel on the roadway.

_____ 10. You conclude you need to reduce speed.

Identify the HTS Category

Check the box to the right that best identifies
each item in the list below.

1. tractor-semitrailer
2. bicyclist
3. YIELD sign
4. Greyhound bus
5. freeway
6. student driver
7. gravel road
8. school parking lot
9. jogger
10. train
11. passenger
12. school bus
13. rural route
14. camping trailer
15. traffic light

	People	Vehicles	Roadways
1.			
2.			
3.			
4.			
5.			
6.			
7.			
8.			
9.			
10.			
11.			
12.			
13.			
14.			
15.			

Your Driving Responsibilities

Match each statement with a category of responsibility listed in
the box.

financial responsibility	environmental responsibility
legal responsibility	responsibility to self and others

_____ 1. Responsible drivers strive to behave respectfully toward other
drivers.

_____ 2. You must stop if you are involved in a collision.

_____ 3. Operating, fixed, and crash costs are part of owning and driving a
vehicle.

_____ 4. All drivers should try to buy and maintain fuel-efficient vehicles
and use fuel-efficient driving habits.

_____ 5. As a driver, you must obey all traffic laws.

Name _____ Date _____

Select the Driving Task

Check the box to the right that identifies each item in the list below.

	Mental Skills (make decisions)	Physical Skills (control the car)	Social Skills (interact with others)
1.			
2.			
3.			
4.			
5.			
6.			
7.			
8.			
9.			
10.			
11.			
12.			

1. Shows courtesy to a pedestrian
2. Identifies traffic signs
3. Negotiates a sharp turn
4. Judges the space around the vehicle
5. Uses the IPDE Process
6. Joins car pools
7. Drives while tired
8. Yields to the other driver
9. Turns on the windshield wipers
10. Shakes a fist at another driver
11. Predicts the light will turn red
12. Shifts into another gear

Test Your Knowledge and Attitude

Check true or false for each statement below.

	True	False
1.		
2.		
3.		
4.		
5.		
6.		
7.		
8.		
9.		
10.		
11.		
12.		
13.		
14.		
15.		

1. You are responsible for avoiding trouble.
2. Your attitude toward life and driving will not affect your driving.
3. Driving is a risk that can be reduced by using good habits.
4. It's not my fault if I lose control of my car on a dark roadway.
5. My friends don't wear safety belts, so I shouldn't either.
6. Being a good driver takes time and practice.
7. Responsible drivers buy fuel-efficient cars.
8. Safe drivers are usually "wimps."
9. Air crashes kill more people than vehicle collisions.
10. Responsible, low-risk drivers are the most important part of the HTS.
11. Decision-making skills are not as important as physical skills.
12. Rain, nighttime, or rough pavement can become major problems.
13. Traffic jams are unavoidable; no one is responsible for them.
14. It's best to put distance between yourself and angry drivers.
15. Following too closely is a major cause of collisions.

Identify the Graduated Driver Licensing Program Stage

Check the driver licensing stage number shown in the box below that describes the step in the licensing process.

> ① Learner's Permit Stage
> ② Intermediate License Stage
> ③ Full-Privilege License Stage

License Stages		
1. ①	②	③
2. ①	②	③
3. ①	②	③
4. ①	②	③
5. ①	②	③
6. ①	②	③
7. ①	②	③
8. ①	②	③
9. ①	②	③
10. ①	②	③

1. Permitted to drive when supervised by an adult, licensed driver

2. Must have successfully completed an approved driver education course

3. Night driving usually is restricted

4. Complete the intermediate stage violation-free

5. Passengers can be limited in age and/or number

6. Full, unrestricted privileges are earned

7. If the learner has a violation or collision, the "clock" is set back to zero

8. A minimum number of hours of practice driving may be required

9. May be required to complete an advanced driver education course

10. Practice driving may be continued to meet the required hours

Name Ways to Manage Environmental Problems

The management of our transportation-related environmental problems is the responsibility of all drivers. On the blanks below, list ways to meet this responsibility.

_____

_____

_____

_____

_____

Name _____ Date _____

Pick a Word

Use the words in the box below to complete each statement.

advisory speed limit	lane signal	roadway markings
basic speed law	minimum speed limit	school zone
flashing signal	pedestrian signal	shared left-turn
guide sign	regulatory sign	traffic signals
international signs	right-turn-on-red	warning sign

_____ 1. Information on routes, service areas, and points of interest are provided on a _____.

_____ 2. A(n) _____ tells you about the laws that you must obey.

_____ 3. To keep traffic moving, a(n) _____ is set on some primary highways and expressways.

_____ 4. A yellow, diamond-shaped sign that alerts you to possible hazards is called a(n) _____.

_____ 5. Two signs used in a(n) _____ alert drivers to children who might dart out into the street without looking.

_____ 6. Obey the _____ when traffic, roadway, or weather conditions are bad.

_____ 7. To help drivers make safe left turns in the middle of the block, a(n) _____ lane is used in many cities.

_____ 8. Special conditions such as a sharp curve are often posted with a(n) _____ sign.

_____ 9. At some intersections, a(n) _____ alerts drivers to dangerous conditions.

_____ 10. Painted solid lines, broken lines, arrows, or words are called _____.

_____ 11. Changes in travel direction during rush-hour traffic is indicated by a(n) _____ light hanging overhead.

_____ 12. When a traffic signal is red, the _____ law allows a driver to turn right.

_____ 13. Drivers who travel from country to country can understand the meaning of _____ because they use symbols rather than words.

_____ 14. At heavily traveled intersections, a(n) _____ is mounted near traffic lights.

_____ 15. All _____ have specific colors to help traffic flow smoothly.

Match the Color

Use the colors in the box below to identify the highway signs. Write in the blank the color that matches the sign.

red	green	orange	blue	yellow

_____ 1. Construction or detour

_____ 2. Stop, yield, or prohibited

_____ 3. Motorist service

_____ 4. Information on routes and distances

_____ 5. Warning, danger ahead

Check Your Knowledge

Check true or false for each of the situations below.

	True	False
1.		
2.		
3.		
4.		
5.		
6.		
7.		
8.		
9.		
10.		

1. When two drivers stop at the same time at an intersection, the driver on the right should go first.

2. The posted maximum speed limit is safe for any driving conditions.

3. A diamond-shaped sign warns drivers of conditions such as a divided highway or deer crossing.

4. The sign with a black "X" and two "Rs" warns drivers of a railroad crossing ahead.

5. At intersections where a stop line and pedestrian crosswalk are marked, you must stop at the pedestrian crosswalk.

6. Drivers must come to a full stop at a flashing red light.

7. The flashing pedestrian signal alerts drivers to pedestrians in the crosswalk.

8. YIELD signs and STOP signs are examples of regulatory signs.

9. Interstate routes heading east or west are odd-numbered.

10. A yellow pennant-shaped sign and solid yellow line are used in no-passing zones.

Pick the Sign Shape

Write the letter of the sign that matches the description.

A.

B.

C.

D.

E.

F.

G.

H.

I.

_____ 1. This black and white regulatory sign identifies the maximum speed limit.

_____ 2. These signs alert you to possible dangers ahead.

_____ 3. The railroad crossing location is marked with this sign.

_____ 4. This red and white sign means a driver must be ready to yield the right-of-way.

_____ 5. This black and white sign indicates traffic may only flow in one direction.

_____ 6. This sign is placed on the left side of the roadway at the start of a no-passing zone.

_____ 7. When this sign shows a crosswalk with children, it marks a school zone.

_____ 8. A full stop is required at this red and white sign.

_____ 9. This brown sign guides you to public recreation areas.

_____ 10. When this sign is orange it warns of a construction zone.

Name _____ Date _____

Choose the Best Action

Write the letter of the action you would use. You will use some letters more than once.

	Action
A.	Pull off the roadway immediately
B.	Maintain position
C.	Reduce speed
D.	Come to a full stop
E.	Change lanes
F.	Continue in your lane
G.	Proceed with caution
H.	Steer toward the center of the roadway
I.	Yield to the other driver

_____ 1. The road is divided with two solid yellow lines and you want to pass.

_____ 2. You see red raised roadway markers in the road ahead.

_____ 3. You are traveling at the maximum speed limit and it starts snowing.

_____ 4. There is no other traffic as you approach a red flashing light.

_____ 5. You are traveling at 35 mph when you see a school zone sign.

_____ 6. A two-way roadway is divided by a shared left-turn lane and you want to turn left.

_____ 7. The roadway in your lane has a left-turn arrow. You want to turn right.

_____ 8. The traffic light turns yellow as you enter the intersection.

_____ 9. The traffic light is green but a traffic control officer is signaling you to stop.

_____ 10. Driving late at night you feel rumble strips under your tires.

_____ 11. You are traveling in the far right lane. The sign ahead warns you that the lane is ending.

_____ 12. You approach an intersection with a flashing yellow light.

_____ 13. You arrive at a four-way stop at the same time as the driver to the right.

_____ 14. The lane you are traveling in has a green arrow pointing toward your intended path of travel.

Use the Pictures

Identify the signs and check the correct category for each below.

Sign	Regulatory	Warning	Guide
1.			
2.			
3.			
4.			
5.			
6.			

1.

3.

5.

2.

4.

6.

Study the Pictures

For each picture, write the action you would take in the situation.

You are in the left lane entering this construction area. You slowed
to the posted speed limit. What else should you have done?

_____

Where do you stop?

_____

You want to turn right. Which lanes permit a right turn?

_____

Pick a Word

Use the word or words in the box below that matches each statement.

accelerator pedal	hazard flasher control
Antilock Braking System light	head restraint
brake pedal	hood-release lever
clutch	odometer
cruise control	shift indicator

_____ 1. This indicates the antilock braking system is functioning.

_____ 2. This optional device allows you to set a constant speed in your vehicle.

_____ 3. The driver controls the speed of the vehicle with this device.

_____ 4. This padded safety device helps reduce whiplash injuries in a collision.

_____ 5. Use this device to warn other drivers of a vehicle breakdown or problem.

_____ 6. You must have your foot on this device when shifting from parking gear to a driving gear.

_____ 7. This gauge on the instrument panel shows the number of miles a vehicle has been driven.

_____ 8. You must use this device before checking or replacing any engine fluids.

_____ 9. This device allows the driver to change gears when driving a vehicle with a manual transmission.

_____ 10. This device indicates the gear being used by the driver or the need to change to a higher gear.

Write the Basic Vehicle Operation Term

Write the terms for the definitions below on the blank lines provided.

_____ 1. The point at which the brakes begin to slow the vehicle

_____ 2. An area that may not be visible to the driver when looking in the rearview or sideview mirrors

_____ 3. Effectively using vision and a comfortable and balanced hand position to point the vehicle in the direction you want to drive

_____ 4. Looking far ahead in the middle of your intended path of travel

_____ 5. In a vehicle without ABS, when the brakes are applied with such force that the wheels stop turning and the tires begin to slide on the pavement

Write the Warning Information

The names of critical instrument panel warning lights and gauges (as shown in the picture) appear below. Fill in the vehicle information the driver receives from each device.

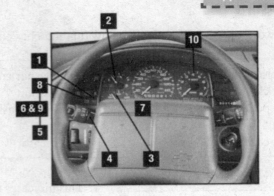

1. Safety belt alert light: _____

2. Fuel gauge: _____

3. Temperature warning light or gauge (H): _____

4. Oil pressure warning light: _____

5. Air bag warning light: _____

6. Parking brake warning light: _____

7. Left and right signals flashing: _____

8. ABS alert light: _____

9. Brake system warning light: _____

10. Tachometer: _____

Test Your Knowledge

Check correct or incorrect for each statement below.

1. When the oil pressure warning light goes on with the engine running, it indicates that the oil needs changing.

2. The last thing you should do before moving a vehicle away from the curb is release the parking brake.

3. The ABS alert light indicates a problem with the antilock braking system if it comes on while you are driving.

4. If the brake warning light comes on as you apply the foot-brake pedal, it indicates that the brake pads are worn out.

5. In an automatic transmission vehicle, always come to a stop before changing from DRIVE to REVERSE or OVERDRIVE to PARK gears.

6. It will be easier to learn good manual transmission skills after you learn basic vehicle maneuvers.

7. A driver has less control over the power applied in a vehicle with a manual transmission.

8. The driver can start the vehicle in NEUTRAL or PARK gears, regardless of the transmission type.

9. Beginning drivers often try to correct steering errors by moving the steering wheel too much and looking where the car is going.

10. The windshield wipers and washer usually are operated by a switch mounted on the turn-signal lever.

	Correct	Incorrect
1.		
2.		
3.		
4.		
5.		
6.		
7.		
8.		
9.		
10.		

Name _____ Date _____

Use the Picture

Use the picture at the right to answer the vehicle control procedures questions below.

1. What error is this person making in approaching and entering this vehicle? _____

    _____

2. Why is the correct procedure a safer way to enter?

    _____

    _____

3. What outside checks should this person make?

    _____

    _____

Exiting the Vehicle

Number the following steps that a driver should complete when leaving a vehicle from the driver's side.

_____ check for traffic   _____ set the parking brake

_____ close the windows   _____ shift to PARK

_____ lock the door   _____ turn off the headlights

_____ take your foot off the brake   _____ turn off the ignition

_____ open the door and exit   _____ walk to the rear of the vehicle

Identify the Gear

For each situation listed, check the gear that you should use on an automatic transmission vehicle to complete the maneuver.

1. Backing out of a parking space
2. Driving on an open, level highway
3. Leaving the vehicle in a garage
4. Pulling a heavy load or driving down a very steep hill
5. Driving in the city in moderate snow conditions
6. Restarting the vehicle while moving forward
7. Reducing speed on a low-traction surface prior to making a turn at an intersection

	P	R	N	D	L2	L1
1.						
2.						
3.						
4.						
5.						
6.						
7.						

Name _____ Date _____

Use the Picture

Study the controls in the picture to the right and read each driver action below. Write in the boxes the number and name of the control to use.

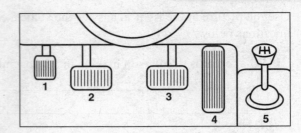

1. In a manual transmission vehicle, the driver must push this pedal when stopping and changing gears.

2. The driver must use these devices to change gears.

3. The driver must use this device to slow or stop the vehicle.

4. The driver must use this device when preparing to leave the vehicle.

5. The driver must use this pedal to increase speed or change speed of the engine.

	Number	Name
1.		
2.		
3.		
4.		
5.		

Answer the Question

Use the word or words in the box that best answer the questions below.

brake pedal	OVERDRIVE
clutch	PARK
DRIVE	REVERSE
lower gears	semi-automatic transmission
NEUTRAL	

1. When slowing before a sharp turn, what pedal can you use to gain added control?

2. Which gear would you use to move forward from a stop?

3. Which gear would you use to back out of a garage?

4. Your vehicle allows you to shift gears manually without the use of a clutch. What kind of transmission do you have?

5. You are towing a heavy trailer. What gear(s) can you use to send more power to your wheels?

6. What gear locks the transmission?

7. Your engine stalls while you are driving. To what gear should you shift?

8. What gear can be used for forward driving, but also saves fuel?

9. You are slowing your vehicle from higher speeds. What vehicle-control device would you use?

10. You are changing gears or slowing your vehicle from slow speeds in a manual transmission. What vehicle-control device would you use?

1. _____

2. _____

3. _____

4. _____

5. _____

6. _____

7. _____

8. _____

9. _____

10. _____

Pick a Word

Use the word or words in the box that matches each definition below.

angle parking	perpendicular parking
convex mirror	personal reference point
forward reference point	reference point
hill parking	standard reference point
parallel parking	turnabout

_____ 1. Parallel parking where the front wheels are turned to prevent the vehicle from rolling downhill when left unattended

_____ 2. Parking at a right angle to the curb

_____ 3. A maneuver used to turn your vehicle around so you can go in the opposite direction

_____ 4. Allows the driver a wider view of the side and rear of the vehicle

_____ 5. Parking that requires a space about six feet longer than the vehicle being parked

_____ 6. When steering should begin during a maneuver

_____ 7. Parking diagonally to a curb

_____ 8. Some part of the outside or inside of the vehicle, as viewed from the driver's seat, that relates to some part of the roadway

_____ 9. A reference point on the vehicle typically used by most drivers

_____ 10. A unique part on a vehicle sometimes used by drivers as a reference point

Use the Picture

Study pictures A, B, C, and D below and draw solid lines over the dotted lines showing the correct front wheel position for each parking situation.

A. Uphill with a curb   B. Uphill with no curb   C. Downhill with a curb   D. Downhill with no curb

Test Your Knowledge

Check correct or incorrect for each statement below.

1. In order to drive in a straight line either forward or backward, hold the steering wheel as steady as possible.

2. When backing in a straight line, move the top of the steering wheel in the direction you want the back of the vehicle to go.

3. To check for a vehicle in the mirror's blind spot, you can look over your shoulder in the direction you wish to move.

4. A common error in lane changing is using lane positions 1 and 3.

5. When planning a turn, signal at least five seconds in advance.

6. When backing to the right, allow a wide space on the right because the front of the vehicle will swing to the right.

7. A U-turn is risky because several lanes of traffic must be crossed to execute the turn.

8. When changing lanes, it is not necessary to make a blind-spot check if you have checked your rearview and sideview mirrors.

9. The driver of a vehicle leaving a parallel parking space must yield to all approaching traffic.

10. A three-point turnabout should only be used on a dead-end street or a rural roadway with no driveways.

	Correct	Incorrect
1.		
2.		
3.		
4.		
5.		
6.		
7.		
8.		
9.		
10.		

Identify the Turnabout

_____

_____

_____

_____

_____

1. Which turnabout requires a wide space because no backing is done?

2. Which turnabout is used when there is a driveway on the right and no traffic behind?

3. Which turnabout requires you to back across two lanes of traffic?

4. Which turnabout requires that you back into the traffic flow before moving forward?

5. Which turnabout requires that you stop your car across traffic lanes?

back into the driveway on the right side
three-point turnabout
pull into the driveway on left or right side
mid-block U-turn
pull into the driveway on the right side

Use the Diagrams

A: Left lane change

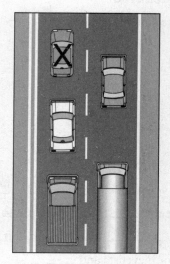

B: Right lane change

C

For diagrams A and B, circle the vehicle that is in the blind spot of vehicle X.

For diagram C, draw an arrow to show the correct turn path for Vehicle A and Vehicle B. Vehicle A is turning right. Vehicle B is turning left.

Pick the Hand and Arm Positions

Read each driving maneuver below. Write the letter of the correct hand and arm position that best matches each statement.

_____ **1.** Steering straight backward

_____ **2.** Changing lanes

_____ **3.** Begin backing to the right

_____ **4.** Signaling with hand for the left turn

_____ **5.** Checking right blind spot

_____ **6.** Begin backing to the left

_____ **7.** Checking the left blind spot

_____ **8.** Signaling with hand for right turn

_____ **9.** Signaling with hand to slow or stop

_____ **10.** Preparing to begin parallel park (right side)

_____ **11.** Exiting a parallel parking space on the left side of a one-way street

_____ **12.** Crossing a railroad track

Hand and Arm Positions
A. right hand on steering wheel, left arm extended straight out
B. right hand on steering wheel, left arm extended out and up
C. right hand on steering wheel, left arm out and down
D. both hands on the steering wheel in a balanced position
E. left hand on steering wheel, right arm on top of the seat

Name _____ Date _____

Complete the Statements on Turning Procedures

Write the word shown in the box that completes the statements for turning procedures below.

accelerate	front
brake	left
center	nearest
correct	pedestrians
crosswalk	traffic

_____ 1. Position your vehicle in the _____ lane.

_____ 2. Apply gentle _____ pressure to reduce speed.

_____ 3. Check _____ to front, rear, left, and right zones.

_____ 4. Search for bicyclists and _____.

_____ 5. Slow to about 10 mph just before a _____.

_____ 6. For a right turn, check to the _____ again before turning.

_____ 7. Turn the steering wheel when your vehicle's _____ wheels are even with the bend of the corner.

_____ 8. For a left turn, make a check right, then left. Turn the steering wheel just before you reach the ____ of the intersection.

_____ 9. Turn into the _____ lane of traffic going in your direction.

_____ 10. Then _____ about halfway through the turn.

Use the Picture

Study the picture and answer the parking questions below.

1. Before entering the parking space, how far should vehicles A and B be positioned from the parked vehicles on their right?

_____

2. Vehicle C is about to begin backing into the parking stall. How much distance should there be between vehicle C and the vehicle on its right?

_____

3. Give two ways vehicles A, B, and C should communicate their intentions.

_____

4. Before backing into the parking stall, which bumper should vehicle C use to line up with the parked vehicle on its right?

_____

5. When exiting, when should the driver of vehicle B begin to turn the vehicle's wheels?

_____

_____

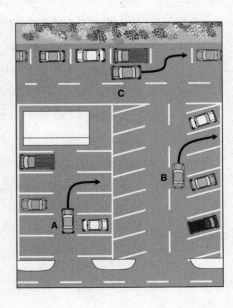

Name _____ Date _____

Pick a Word

Use the word or words in the box below that matches each definition.

4–6 second range	line of sight	selective seeing
12–15 second range	minimize a hazard	separate hazards
central vision	open zone	space cushion
closed zone	orderly visual search pattern	target area
compromise space	path of travel	traction
escape path	peripheral vision	zones
field of vision	scanning	

_____ 1. Place to go in case of possible conflict

_____ 2. Process of searching critical areas in a regular sequence

_____ 3. Six areas of space around the vehicle

_____ 4. The space your vehicle will occupy

_____ 5. A space where you can drive free of restrictions to your line of sight or path of travel

_____ 6. Area of space around the vehicle that is free of restrictions, hazards, and conflicts when you use it

_____ 7. All of the area that is visible to the driver when looking straight ahead

_____ 8. A space not open because of restrictions in your line of sight or path of travel

_____ 9. Give as much space as possible to the greater hazard

_____ 10. Reducing risk by putting more distance between yourself and the hazard

_____ 11. The gripping power between the tire and the road surface

_____ 12. Selecting and identifying only those clues for restrictions, hazards, or conflicts that are important to your driving task

_____ 13. Area far ahead in your path of travel and the area to the left and right

_____ 14. The recommended searching area for identifying changes in your line of sight and path of travel

_____ 15. The part of a field of vision surrounding the central vision

_____ 16. The searching range where you need to get the final update of how you are controlling your intended path of travel

_____ 17. When the driver follows the process of an orderly visual search pattern

_____ 18. Adjusting your speed in order to handle one hazard at a time

_____ 19. That part of a field of vision where you can see clearly and sharply

_____ 20. The distance you can see ahead in the direction you are looking

Name _____ Date _____

Use the Picture

You are driving and observe the traffic scene shown on the right.
Read the statements below. Think about which step of the IPDE
Process—identify, predict, decide, or execute—applies to each.
Write the letter (I, P, D, or E) in the blank before each statement.

_____ 1. A vehicle may come over the crest of the hill into
your lane.

_____ 2. There is a STOP sign ahead.

_____ 3. There is a restriction to your line of sight and path of
travel.

_____ 4. You apply the foot brake, slow, and move to lane position 3.

_____ 5. A vehicle crosses the center line and closes your left-front zone as it crests the hill, so you will
slow and move to the right to avoid a collision.

Write the Terms Associated with IPDE Process

The list below shows the four steps of the IPDE Process. On the
blank lines, write the terms from the box below that refer to each
part of the IPDE Process.

accelerating	control of your vehicle
actions of other roadway users	line-of-sight restrictions
braking	other roadway users
change direction	path-of-travel restrictions
change speed	roadway features and conditions
closed or open zones	signaling
communicate with others	steering
consequences of your actions	traffic controls

IDENTIFY (look for)

1. _____

2. _____

3. _____

4. _____

5. _____

6. _____

PREDICT (risk of possible consequences)

7. _____

8. _____

9. _____

DECIDE (avoid conflict)

10. _____

11. _____

12. _____

EXECUTE (reduce conflict options)

13. _____

14. _____

15. _____

16. _____

Use the IPDE Process to Separate Hazards

When faced with two restrictions, hazards, or conditions, try to separate the problems so you can handle only one restriction, hazard, or condition at a time. Look at the picture on the right and answer the questions in the table below.

What are the two restrictions, hazards, or conditions that need to be separated in the picture?	1. _____ 2. _____
What would you need to predict in this situation?	3. _____ _____
What is your decision to separate the hazards present?	4. _____ _____
What action should you take to separate the hazards?	5. _____ _____

Test Your Knowledge

You are the driver of vehicle X in the expressway merge diagram on the left. Check the step of the IPDE Process that best describes the action(s) you are taking in each statement below.

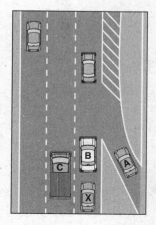

1. Vehicle A is approaching from the entrance ramp.
2. Vehicle A may merge into your path of travel.
3. There is no vehicle behind vehicle C.
4. Vehicle B is maintaining speed, while vehicle C is accelerating.
5. You are too close to vehicle B.
6. You will slow and change lanes so vehicle A can merge.
7. You check the mirrors and slow.
8. You will need to signal before changing lanes.
9. You signal, check traffic, and move into the center lane.
10. You cancel your signal.

	I	P	D	E
1.				
2.				
3.				
4.				
5.				
6.				
7.				
8.				
9.				
10.				

Match the Means of Communication

Review the various means of communication listed on the right.
Write the letter of the means that best matches each driving situation
below.

_____ 1. Move to the right in your lane

_____ 2. Need to warn a vehicle that is straying into your lane

_____ 3. Car with high-beam headlights on is approaching

_____ 4. Plan to turn left at next corner

_____ 5. Watch other drivers at 4-way stop

_____ 6. Want to be seen from the rear at night

_____ 7. Parked at curb at night

_____ 8. Car breakdown in a traffic lane

_____ 9. Backing out of a parking space

_____ 10. Preparing to stop at an intersection

A. back-up lights
B. brake lights
C. lane position 3
D. hazard flasher lights
E. eye contact or body movement
F. high- and low-beam headlights
G. horn
H. parking lights
I. taillights
J. turn-signal lights

Use the IPDE Process

Study the driving situation at the right. You are driving vehicle X. Use your selective seeing process to identify restrictions, hazards, or conflicts. In the columns on the left, check whether each restriction, hazard, or
conflict is a high or low priority. Give a reason for each on the line below.

	PRIORITY	
	HIGH	LOW
1.		
2.		
3.		
4.		
5.		
6.		
7.		
8.		
9.		
10.		

1. Bicyclist
_____
2. Oncoming car ahead
_____
3. Vehicle in driveway at the left
_____
4. Truck parked up ahead on left
_____
5. Vehicle near intersection ahead
_____
6. Tractor by intersection
_____
7. Oncoming car stopped at intersection
_____
8. Truck behind you
_____
9. House on the right
_____
10. Pedestrian on left near roadway
_____

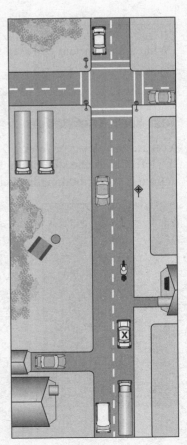

Pick a Word

Use the word or words from the box that matches each definition below.

carbon monoxide	glare resistance
color blindness	night blindness
depth perception	speed smear
emotions	tunnel vision
glare recovery time	visual acuity

_____ **1.** Not being able to see well at night

_____ **2.** Not being able to tell one color from another

_____ **3.** Narrow field of side vision (a total of 140 degrees or less)

_____ **4.** Ability to judge the distance between yourself and other objects

_____ **5.** Time your eyes need to regain clear vision after being affected by bright lights

_____ **6.** Ability to see things clearly near and far away

_____ **7.** Strong feelings such as anger, fear, or joy that influence the way you think and act

_____ **8.** Colorless and odorless gas that is part of a vehicle's exhaust fumes

_____ **9.** The ability to continue seeing when looking at bright lights

_____ **10.** The blur of objects off to your sides as your speed increases

Correct the Incorrect Statements

Check if the underlined word or words in each statement below are correct or incorrect. If incorrect, write the correct words in the box to the right.

1. A person with normal visual acuity has 20/20 vision.

2. Most states require a minimum visual acuity of 20/20 to drive.

3. Your peripheral vision provides you with your clearest vision.

4. If you must wear glasses to pass the vision test, you need not wear them driving.

5. Your fringe vision is used to detect changes in your rearview mirror.

6. The closer to the central vision, the less clear the view.

	Correct	Incorrect	Correct Words
1.			
2.			
3.			
4.			
5.			
6.			

Name _____ Date _____

Identify the Disability

For each situation below, check the disability that most
likely contributed to each situation.

1. Driver runs off the roadway after meeting a vehicle
   using high-beam headlights.

2. Driver sideswipes two parked cars when driving on a
   narrow street.

3. In daylight, vehicle hits bicyclist coming out of a
   driveway.

4. Driver collides head-on while passing a truck.

5. Driver leaves brightly lighted shopping center and
   misses the first curve.

6. Driver hits a car pulling out of a driveway on the
   right side.

7. Driver misjudges the distance barrier ahead, slams
   on the brakes, and is rear-ended.

8. On a bright sunny day, driver hits a pedestrian in a
   crosswalk.

	Poor Depth Perception	Narrow Field of Vision	Poor Glare Recovery
1.			
2.			
3.			
4.			
5.			
6.			
7.			
8.			

Choose the Greater Risk

For each pair of risks, choose whether risk A or risk B is the greater
risk.

	Risk A	Risk B		Greater Risk A	B
1.	Driving on an expressway	Driving on a busy two-lane roadway	1.		
2.	Driving at night	Driving in the daytime	2.		
3.	Driving on a quiet street	Driving in heavy city traffic	3.		
4.	Driving when you are calm	Driving when you are angry	4.		
5.	Driving when you are tired	Driving when you are rested	5.		
6.	Driving in the rain	Driving on dry pavement	6.		
7.	Driving in a strange car	Driving in a familiar car	7.		
8.	Driving with passengers who know you are a careful driver	Driving with passengers who encourage you to hurry	8.		
9.	Driving when you are in a hurry	Driving when you have allowed extra time	9.		
10.	Challenge an aggressive driver	Yield to an aggressive driver	10.		

chapter 6

Choose the Driving Deficiency

Check if the information below helps compensate for color-blindness, depth perception, or glare recovery.

1. When driving at night, avoid looking directly at bright lights.

2. Remember that red is on the top or the left on signal lights.

3. If you are temporarily blinded, slow or stop until your vision clears.

4. Allow for an extra clear distance ahead before passing.

5. Read signs that appear with flashing lights and other traffic signals.

6. Use the right edge of the roadway as a guide when headlights cause you to look away.

7. Use a known distance, such as a city block, to judge distances.

8. Anticipate blinding situations and glance away.

9. Check all traffic carefully before proceeding at traffic signals.

10. Wear sunglasses and use your vehicle's visor in bright sunlight.

	Color-Blindness	Depth Perception	Glare Recovery
1.			
2.			
3.			
4.			
5.			
6.			
7.			
8.			
9.			
10.			

Use the Picture

Study the picture and answer the question. You are driving down the street when the driver of the white car pulls into your lane and slows down. What should you do?

_____

_____

Check Your Skill With Risk and the Driving Task

Check if each statement below is associated with medicine, carbon monoxide, or emotions.

1. Check your vehicle's exhaust system often.

2. Excitement and happiness can prevent you from fully concentrating on your driving task.

3. Most drivers experience anger more often than any other feeling.

4. Ask your pharmacist or physician about any side effects.

5. You might feel panic-stricken in an unfamiliar, difficult situation.

6. Other drivers interfere with your planned speed or path of travel.

7. Avoid running your vehicle's engine inside a closed area.

8. Read the label before taking and before deciding whether or not to drive.

9. Anger can impair your ability to brake, steer, and accelerate smoothly.

10. Discourage passengers in your car from smoking.

11. If taken to relieve headache pain or hay fever, it may also reduce your alertness.

12. In traffic jams, turn off heater or air conditioner fan.

13. Sorrow, depression, and anxiety can adversely affect driving.

14. Be alert for drivers who are stressed by driving in rush-hour traffic.

15. Avoid driving with the rear windows of the vehicle open.

	Medicine	Carbon Monoxide	Emotions
1.			
2.			
3.			
4.			
5.			
6.			
7.			
8.			
9.			
10.			
11.			
12.			
13.			
14.			
15.			

Name _____ Date _____

Pick a Word

Use the word or words in the box that matches each definition below.

blood alcohol concentration (BAC)	inhibitions
depressant	intoxilyzer
designated driver	nystagmus
driving under the influence (DUI)/ driving while intoxicated (DWI)	over-the-counter medicine (OTC)
	peer education
euphoria	peer pressure
field sobriety test	prescription medicine
hallucinogen	stimulant
implied-consent law	zero-tolerance law

_____ 1. Inner forces of personality that hold back one's impulsive behavior

_____ 2. Percentage of alcohol in a person's bloodstream determined by chemical tests

_____ 3. Infraction a driver with a BAC of 0.08 can be charged with

_____ 4. A drug that slows down the central nervous system

_____ 5. On-the-spot roadside tests that help a police officer detect driver impairment from alcohol

_____ 6. Drugs that can be obtained legally without a doctor's order

_____ 7. Where young people help other young people make responsible decisions

_____ 8. A mind-altering drug that changes a personality and distorts vision and perception

_____ 9. A drug that speeds up a person's central nervous system

_____ 10. Machine that determines BAC by measuring a person's breath

_____ 11. Drugs that can only be purchased under a doctor's order

_____ 12. A person's alcohol-induced false feeling of well-being

_____ 13. A law that makes it illegal for persons under 21 to drive with any measurable amount of alcohol in the blood

_____ 14. The influence that others of similar age and/or interests have on another person

_____ 15. By accepting a driver's license, a person agrees to be tested for BAC if stopped for suspicion of alcohol or drug use while driving.

_____ 16. The involuntary jerking of the eyes as a person gazes to the side

_____ 17. Decides ahead of time to abstain from drinking at social functions

Test Your Knowledge

Check myth or fact for each statement below.

1. A person can burn off alcohol by strenuous activity.
2. A person will be affected by drinking beer.
3. A person will not drive as well after a few alcoholic drinks.
4. Alcohol will not affect a person who has built up a tolerance.
5. A person can sober up by drinking black coffee and taking a cold shower.

	Myth	Fact
1.		
2.		
3.		
4.		
5.		

Study the Statements

Check correct or incorrect for each of the following statements about peer pressure.

1. Peer pressure is not influential in your decision-making process.
2. Cheering for your school's football team is an example of positive peer pressure.
3. Peer pressure only affects young people.
4. Responsible decisions can help you be in control of your life.
5. Peer education is a process in which young people help other young people make decisions.
6. You have no responsibilities toward friends who decide to drink and drive.
7. There is nothing you can do to prevent underage drinking problems.
8. A designated driver should not drink any alcoholic beverages.
9. Maturity and independent thinking can help you resist peer pressure.
10. If you know that the person who is supposed to drive you home has had a few alcoholic beverages, you should make alternate plans.

	Correct	Incorrect
1.		
2.		
3.		
4.		
5.		
6.		
7.		
8.		
9.		
10.		

List the Factors

List below the main factors that determine the degree of impairment caused by consumption of alcohol.

_____

_____

_____

_____

Identify the Type of Drug

Identify the type of drug shown in the box that causes each effect on
the body listed below.

depressant	marijuana
hallucinogen	stimulant

_____ 1. Slows down the body's mental and physical processes

_____ 2. Reduces abilities to judge distance, time, and direction

_____ 3. Causes a person to lose inhibitions

_____ 4. Speeds up the body's central nervous system

_____ 5. Impairs judgement, memory, depth perception, and coordination

_____ 6. Causes reflex actions of the body to slow down

_____ 7. Gives feelings of energy and alertness at first

_____ 8. Alters personality and causes panic

_____ 9. Slows down the body's central nervous system

_____ 10. After alertness wears off, causes person to become tired quickly

Study the Statements

Check correct or incorrect for each statement.

		Correct	Incorrect
1.	Alcohol is the most commonly used drug in our society.		
2.	Nearly half of those killed in alcohol-related collisions were not drinking.		
3.	When alcohol is combined with other drugs, the effects of both can be multiplied.		
4.	More than half of all fatalities during holidays are alcohol related.		
5.	Teenage and adult drinking differ in that adults do more drinking in vehicles.		
6.	All states enforce a minimum drinking age of 21.		
7.	The greatest hazard young people face is driving and riding with other drivers.		
8.	The highest rates of intoxication are found in drivers in their forties.		
9.	A person who serves alcohol to an intoxicated individual may be held responsible for damages caused by that individual.		
10.	One drink of alcohol does not always affect the behavior of some people.		

Use the Picture

Read the statements below about this picture of a collision. Check true or false for each statement.

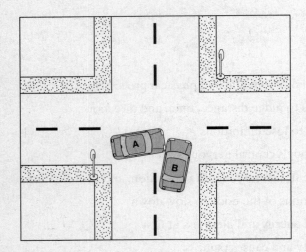

	True	False
1.		
2.		
3.		
4.		
5.		

1. The breath of Driver A smells of alcohol. This is proof for a DUI conviction.

2. If arrested for DWI, Driver A or B will most likely be asked to take a breath test under the implied-consent law.

3. If Driver A has a history of heavy drinking, it is less likely that his/her driving actions would have caused the collision.

4. Driver A could be convicted of DUI if he or she has a BAC above 0.08 in tests given right after the collision.

5. If Driver A refuses to be tested for BAC and is not convicted of DWI, his or her driver's license cannot be suspended.

Check Alcohol-Affected Behavior

Check whether each alcohol-affected behavior below is likely to occur in the average person after having one, three, or four alcoholic drinks in one hour.

	Drinks in an Hour		
	One	**Three**	**Four**
1.			
2.			
3.			
4.			
5.			

1. Most of a person's behaviors are affected. Body parts seem not to work together. Walking without stumbling is difficult.

2. Judgment and reasoning are not reliable. Person may do or say things that are rude and unreasonable.

3. Hearing, speech, vision, and balance are affected. Ability to drive is greatly impaired.

4. Inhibitions are lessened. Person may be less critical of oneself and others.

5. Pupils of the eyes do not become smaller quickly enough as bright light approaches and are slower to open after the bright light passes.

Pick a Word

Use the word or words in the box that best matches each definition below.

auditory distraction	gawking
biomechanical distraction	projectile
cognitive distraction	rubbernecking
distracted driving	visual distraction
driver inattention	

_____ **1.** When a person continually looks all around the scene of a crash or fire

_____ **2.** You are not focusing mentally on the primary task of driving

_____ **3.** When a driver's awareness and focus drift to anything other than the driving task

_____ **4.** Anything that causes you to take your eyes off the roadway ahead

_____ **5.** When an event, person, activity, or object draws a driver's attention away from the driving task

_____ **6.** Any distraction caused by sounds

_____ **7.** Flying objects that could be a hazard to a driver or passenger

_____ **8.** Any mechanical act not specifically related to driving that is performed by a driver

_____ **9.** When a person stares

Match the Distraction

Match the categories of distraction in the box below to each example.

auditory distractions	cognitive distractions
biomechanical distractions	visual distractions

_____ **1.** Pushing a button or turning a dial

_____ **2.** Holding a conversation with a passenger

_____ **3.** A billboard

_____ **4.** A crying child or a siren

_____ **5.** Eating

_____ **6.** Picking up a CD

_____ **7.** A large dog blocking your rearview mirror

_____ **8.** Your favorite song on the radio

_____ **9.** Colorful street performers

_____ **10.** Thinking about what you will wear to a party

Test Your Knowledge

Check correct or incorrect for each situation. If the statement is
incorrect, write the word or words that would make the statement
correct.

1. Driver distraction does not necessarily deal with a specific event.

2. There are four categories of distraction.

3. Driver inattention is a major factor in most crashes and near-crashes.

4. A person can multitask and still focus enough on the driving task to be a low-risk driver.

5. If you are fatigued, stop and stretch, or switch drivers.

6. Manipulating your cell phone can possibly fall into all four categories of distraction.

7. If you are already in traffic and notice an insect in your car, brake immediately.

8. Eating or drinking while driving can create both visual and biomechanical distractions.

9. Gawking that causes a traffic backlog is only a minor distraction.

10. Novice drivers are less likely to be distracted by passengers than experienced drivers.

	Correct	Incorrect	Corrections
1.			
2.			
3.			
4.			
5.			
6.			
7.			
8.			
9.			
10.			

Reduce Distractions Inside the Vehicle

List five examples of how to reduce inside-the-vehicle distractions.

1. _____

2. _____

3. _____

4. _____

5. _____

Name _____ Date _____

Use the Charts

Use the charts shown to answer the questions below.

Chart A
Cell phone behavior compared by selected demographics

Driver Cell Phone Use as Observed from the Roadside		
	Drivers holding phones to their ears	Drivers speaking with headsets
All Drivers	5%	0.6%
Males	4%	0.4%
Females	6%	0.8%
Apparent Age:		
16–24	8%	0.7%
25–69	4%	0.6%
Drivers with:		
no passengers	6%	0.8%
at least one passenger	2%	0.1%

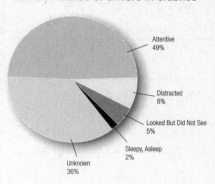

Chart B
Attention status of drivers in crashes

Attentive 49%
Distracted 8%
Looked But Did Not See 5%
Sleepy, Asleep 2%
Unknown 36%

1. What information does chart B measure? _____
   _____

2. Do more drivers hold phones to their ears, or use a headset? _____

3. In chart B, what percentage of drivers was focused on the driving task? _____

4. How does the presence of a passenger affect cell phone use while driving? _____
   _____

5. In chart B, what is the total percentage of drivers who were distracted by a specific event or activity?
   _____

6. Which gender uses the phone more while driving? _____

7. Why do you think younger drivers use cell phones while driving more than older drivers?
   _____

8. In chart B, what do you think is the cause behind the unknown 36 percent?
   _____

Inside or Outside Distractions

Check the box to the right that best applies to each distraction below.

	Inside the Vehicle	Outside the Vehicle
1.		
2.		
3.		
4.		
5.		
6.		
7.		
8.		

1. Street carnival
2. Roadside fire
3. Changing the radio station
4. Talking on your cell phone
5. Wasp on the dashboard
6. Raccoon carcass
7. AMBER alert message board
8. Cluttered back window ledge

Test Your Knowledge

Complete the statements about driver distraction.

_____ 1. Although distracted driving is a form of driver inattention, it differs in that it is usually triggered by some _____.

_____ 2. Drivers have very little, if any, control over _____ distractions.

_____ 3. Drivers can _____ distractions within their vehicles by knowing the locations of controls, securing any objects or pets, avoiding the use of cell phones, and controlling passengers' behaviors.

_____ 4. Driver _____ is often what causes a traffic backlog, not an actual crash.

_____ 5. Safe driving requires drivers to stay _____ on the driving task.

Study the Statements

Check correct or incorrect for each statement.

1. Fatigue is a form of driver inattention.

2. Distraction occurs when a driver chooses to do something that is not necessary to the driving task.

3. You can take your eyes away from the road for up to four seconds and still have enough time to react appropriately to hazards.

4. In some communities, you can face police action for loud music.

5. Driving distraction-free is very easy; most people are just lazy.

	Incorrect	Correct
1.		
2.		
3.		
4.		
5.		

Pick a Word

Use the word or words in the box below to complete each statement.

active restraint device	energy of motion	passive restraint device
banked curve	force of impact	restraint device
blowout	friction	traction
center of gravity	gravity	tread

_____ 1. _____ is the force that pulls vehicles toward the earth.

_____ 2. The gripping action that keeps tires from slipping is _____.

_____ 3. A restraint device, such as an air bag, that works automatically and the occupant does not need to fasten is a(n) _____.

_____ 4. _____ is the friction which allows tires to grip the roadway.

_____ 5. The grooved surface of a tire, called _____, grips the roadway.

_____ 6. A safety belt that a vehicle's occupant must adjust is a(n) _____.

_____ 7. A curve that is higher on the outside is a(n) _____.

_____ 8. The _____ is the force with which one moving object hits another object.

_____ 9. A bald tire might result in a(n) _____, which is a sudden loss of air pressure in the tire.

_____ 10. When an object moves, it uses kinetic energy, which is called _____.

_____ 11. The _____ is a point around which an object's weight is evenly distributed.

_____ 12. Any part of a vehicle that holds an occupant in a collision is a(n) _____.

Complete the Statements on Natural Laws and Vehicle Control

Write the phrase listed in the box that completes each statement on natural laws and vehicle control.

braking distance	reaction distance
perception distance	reaction time
perception time	total stopping distance

_____ 13. The distance your vehicle travels while stopping is _____.

_____ 14. Your _____ is the length of time it takes you to identify, predict, and decide to slow for a hazard.

_____ 15. The distance traveled while you identify a situation is your _____.

_____ 16. Your _____ is the length of time you take to execute your action in response to a hazard after you identify it.

_____ 17. The distance your vehicle travels from the time you apply the brakes until your vehicle stops is called _____.

_____ 18. Your _____ is the distance your vehicle travels while you identify and react to a hazard.

Complete Each Sentence

Write the word or words that complete(s) the following statements.

1. The two forces that work on your vehicle as you go around a curve are inertia and _____.

2. To maintain high levels of traction, the road must be clean, dry, level, and _____
_____

3. Ice tends to form first on areas such as bridges and _____.

4. Check tire pressure when tires are _____.

5. Supplemental restraint systems such as airbags are called _____.

Check Roadways and Tires

Place a check by each of the following items that result in *good* traction.

_____ 1. Ice-covered roadway

_____ 2. Loose-packed gravel roadway

_____ 3. Dry, smooth roadway

_____ 4. Snow tires on snow-covered roadway

_____ 5. Roadway covered with rain

_____ 6. Bald tires

_____ 7. Overinflated tires

_____ 8. Dry, bumpy roadway

_____ 9. Underinflated tires

_____ 10. Tires with wide, deep tread on snow-covered roadway

Use the Picture

Study pictures A, B, and C and answer the questions below about the effects of gravity and speed on vehicles.

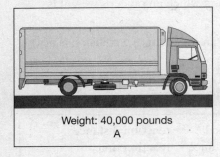

Weight: 40,000 pounds
A

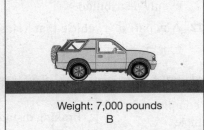

Weight: 7,000 pounds
B

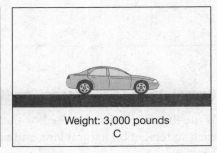

Weight: 3,000 pounds
C

1. Gravity has the greatest effect on the vehicle shown in picture _____.

2. The center of gravity has been raised on the vehicle shown in picture _____.

3. If all three vehicles are traveling at the same speed, is vehicle C's energy of motion *more than* or *less than* that of vehicles A or B? _____

4. When going uphill, will the force of gravity *decrease* or *increase* each vehicle's speed? _____

5. Assume all three vehicles are traveling at 55 mph. They are the same distance from a roadway barrier. Which vehicle will hit the barrier with the greatest force of impact? _____

Use the Picture

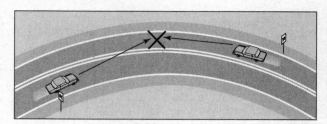

Study the picture. Assume that both cars in the picture are traveling at 55 mph. Both cars have advisory speed signs of 40 mph. Now answer the following questions.

1. Is either car traveling at a safe speed for the curve? _____

2. What kind of energy has each car built up while moving? _____

3. What should each driver have done to avoid a collision at location X? _____

4. What law of nature pulls each car in a straight line toward point X? _____

5. Each car slows to 20 mph. Which law of nature will help keep each car on the roadway? _____
_____

6. Where should each driver have reduced speed to drive through this curve? _____

7. What design of curve would help hold each car on the roadway? _____

8. How much greater would the amount of traction needed be if each car were traveling at 40 mph rather than at 20 mph? _____

9. If the curve was sharper, would each car need *more* or *less* traction? _____

10. At what speed should each driver have been traveling to avoid a collision? _____

Use the Picture

Study each car's position in the picture to the right. Write the letter of the car that best matches each statement.

_____ 1. Stopping distance increases.

_____ 2. Speed increases without accelerating.

_____ 3. The vehicle's center of gravity is raised.

_____ 4. Speed decreases without deceleration.

_____ 5. The force of gravity causes speed to decrease.

_____ 6. Driver has the best clear line of sight ahead and to the rear.

_____ 7. Driver might need to accelerate to maintain speed.

_____ 8. Driver has the greatest line-of-sight restriction.

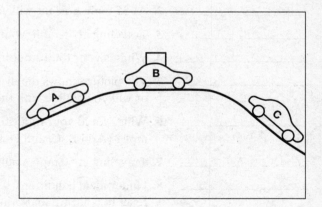

Name _____ Date _____

Estimate the Stopping Distance

Use the charts below and to the right to answer the following questions. You are driving the vehicle at 55 mph.

Use the chart on the right as follows:

- to change miles per hour (A) to feet per second (B)
- to find distance covered in 3/4-second reaction time (C)
- to find approximate braking distance (D)

miles per hour (A)	perception distance per second (B)	3/4-Second reaction distance (C)	approximate braking distance (D)
20	29 ft.	22 ft.	20 ft.
30	44 ft.	33 ft.	40 ft.
40	59 ft.	44 ft.	73 ft.
50	73 ft.	55 ft.	119 ft.
55	81 ft.	61 ft.	150 ft.

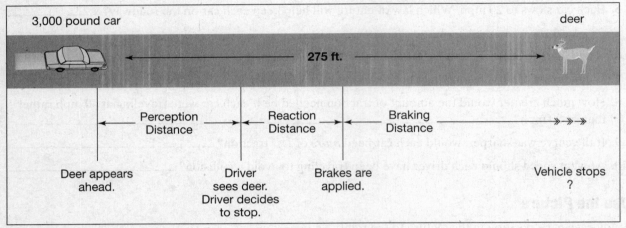

_____ 1. A deer appears ahead. You see the deer *one second* later. How many feet did you travel?

_____ 2. At 55 mph, how far will you travel during your 3/4-second reaction time?

_____ 3. Traveling at 55 mph, your approximate braking distance is how many feet?

_____ 4. What is your total stopping distance? (Add the answers to questions 1, 2, and 3.)

_____ 5. The picture shows the distance between you and the deer. Will you stop in time, or will you collide with the deer?

_____ 6. What would your total stopping distance have been if you were traveling at 50 mph? (Add B, C, and D across in the chart.)

_____ 7. Traveling at 50 mph, could you have avoided colliding with the deer?

_____ 8. Under ideal conditions, what approximate amount of total time do you need to react to a hazard and bring your vehicle to a stop?

_____ 9. What is the most important factor in determining how hard your vehicle will hit the deer?

_____ 10. If your vehicle weighed twice as much, how much harder would your vehicle hit the deer?

Name _____ Date _____

Pick a Word

Use the word or words in the box below to complete each statement.

controlled	fresh green light	right of way
intersection	gap	roundabout
crossbuck	joining traffic	stale green light
delayed green light	point of no return	yielding

_____ **1.** The distance between vehicles on a roadway is known as a _____.

_____ **2.** The privilege of having immediate use of a certain part of the roadway is called _____.

_____ **3.** Letting others go before you is called _____.

_____ **4.** An intersection where signs or a signal assign the right of way is known as a _____.

_____ **5.** A light that has been green for some time is described as a _____.

_____ **6.** A light that has just turned from red to green is called a _____.

_____ **7.** Turning right or left into lanes of other vehicles is called _____.

_____ **8.** The sign before the tracks at a railroad crossing is a _____.

_____ **9.** A light allowing traffic from one side time to turn or go straight before the light for oncoming traffic turns green is known as a _____.

_____ **10.** When several roads meet at a circle, the intersection is a _____.

_____ **11.** When you can no longer stop safely without entering the intersection, you have reached the _____.

Match Each Picture

Study the pictures below. Write the letter for the words that best describe the situation or the type of intersection.

A. controlled intersection	**D.** uncontrolled intersection
B. active railroad crossing	**E.** passive railroad crossing
C. protected left turn	**F.** unprotected left turn

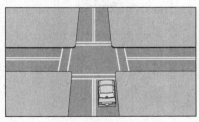

1. _____

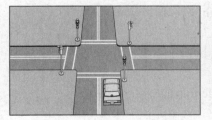

2. _____

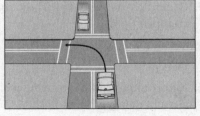

3. _____

4. _____

5. _____

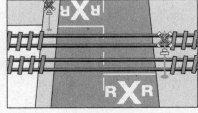

6. _____

Test Your Knowledge

Check true or false for each statement below.

1. When approaching an intersection, you will need to search the left-front, front, and right-front zones to be certain they are open.

2. Treat an uncontrolled intersection the same way you would a STOP sign.

3. You should search the next intersection beginning at least 12 seconds ahead of time.

4. A green light is always an indication to go because it is clear to do so.

5. All controlled intersections have traffic signals that provide for protected left turns.

6. Vehicles leaving a parking lost must yield to all vehicles and pedestrians.

7. Vehicles turning left at uncontrolled intersections must yield to all oncoming vehicles.

8. Traffic controls give vehicles, but not pedestrians, the right of way.

9. Because right turns take less time, they are more dangerous than left turns.

10. You need about two-thirds of a block in each direction to cross an intersection if traffic on the through street is traveling 30 mph.

	True	False
1.		
2.		
3.		
4.		
5.		
6.		
7.		
8.		
9.		
10.		

Answer Each Question

You are approaching an intersection controlled by the traffic signal shown. Check correct or incorrect for each statement.

1. You must stop before reaching the crosswalk.

2. You may turn right after stopping unless a sign prohibits this action.

3. Other drivers should yield the right of way to you when you turn right.

4. You must yield to pedestrians in the crosswalks if you turn right.

5. If oncoming traffic is moving while this light is on, you are at a delayed green light.

	Correct	Incorrect
1.		
2.		
3.		
4.		
5.		

Name _____ Date _____

Use the Picture

Answer the questions below about traffic flow.

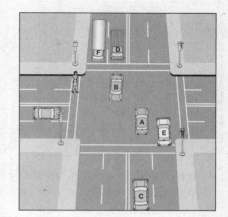

1. Which two vehicles should be given the clear right of way?

   _____

2. Which vehicle, A or B, will turn left first? Explain why.

   _____

3. While waiting to turn, which way should vehicle A's front wheels be pointed? Explain why.

   _____

4. Give two reasons why vehicle A should delay its left turn.

   _____

   _____

5. Both vehicles B and A complete their left turns. Which vehicle, D or C, should be given the right of way? Why?

   _____

   _____

Study the Diagram

Check Yes or No to answer the intersection crossing and joining questions.

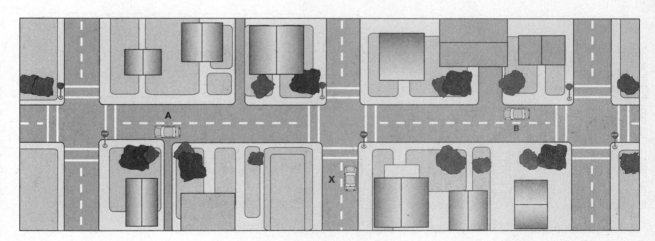

	Yes	No
1.		
2.		
3.		
4.		
5.		

1. Do vehicles A and B have to stop?

2. Should vehicle X be able to cross the intersection safely if vehicles A and B are both traveling at 25 mph?

3. Can vehicle X turn right safely at this time if vehicles A and B are both traveling at 25 mph?

4. Can vehicle X turn left safely at this time if vehicles A and B are both traveling at 30 mph?

5. Vehicle A is traveling at 25 mph and vehicle B is traveling at 30 mph. Should vehicle X attempt to cross the intersection?

Use the Pictures

Answer the questions below.

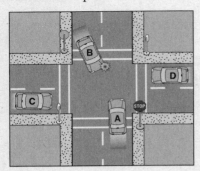

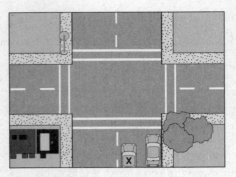

1. Which vehicle, A or B, should be allowed to go first? Give a reason for your choice.

2. Which vehicle, C or D, should go last? Why?

_____

_____

3. When should vehicle D turn right? Why?

_____

_____

4. What type of intersection is this?

_____

5. What hazards make identification of the type of intersection difficult?

_____

_____

6. How might the driver of vehicle X identify the type of intersection?

_____

_____

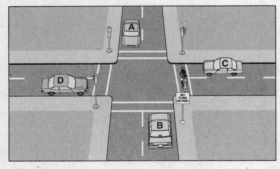

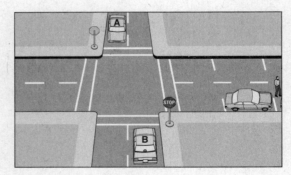

7. What sign prohibits vehicle B from turning?

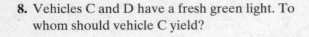

_____

8. Vehicles C and D have a fresh green light. To whom should vehicle C yield?

_____

_____

9. Can vehicle B legally turn right?

_____

_____

10. What conflict might the driver of vehicle B not be able to predict at this point?

_____

_____

Name _____ Date _____

Pick a Word

Use the word or words in the box that completes each statement below.

front brake	low-speed vehicles	scooter
headlight	moped	semi-trailer
helmet	no zones	traction
instability	protective gear	tractor-trailer
jaywalk	reflective	

_____ 1. A motorcycle's small size, handling characteristics, and _____ can cause problems in traffic.

_____ 2. Large blind spots in front, to the sides, and to the rear of a large truck are known as _____.

_____ 3. Even during daylight hours, it's easier for motorists to identify motorcyclists if cyclists have their _____ on.

_____ 4. Helmets, gloves, long sleeves, and pants are examples of ____.

_____ 5. A two-wheeled vehicle that can be driven by a motor or pedal is known as a _____.

_____ 6. A truck that has a powerful tractor that pulls a separate trailer is called a _____.

_____ 7. The _____ provides most of a motorcycle's stopping power.

_____ 8. Some pedestrians _____, or disregard traffic rules and signals.

_____ 9. To be more visible, motorcyclists should wear _____ clothing when riding at night.

_____ 10. The most common size tractor-trailer is called the _____.

_____ 11. A low-powered two-wheeled vehicle that requires no shifting is known as a _____.

_____ 12. Golf carts and other vehicles with top speed between 20 and 25 mph are examples of _____.

_____ 13. Wearing a _____ saves lives, reduces traffic noise, and helps prevent fatigue.

_____ 14. In adverse weather conditions, reduced _____ is far more critical for motorcyclists than for drivers of other types of vehicles.

Name _____ Date _____

Test Your Knowledge

Read the statements below and check whether each motorcyclist's roadway situation is safe or unsafe.

	Safe	Unsafe
1.		
2.		
3.		
4.		
5.		
6.		
7.		
8.		
9.		
10.		

1. Riding in wheel track of a vehicle ahead on a wet roadway
2. Applying the front brake and locking the front wheel
3. Increasing the following distance
4. Riding on a lane line
5. Crossing railroad tracks at a right angle
6. Passing at an intersection
7. Riding side-by-side when making a turn
8. Keeping headlights on at all times
9. Riding in a driver's blind spot
10. Riding between lines of moving vehicles

Study Each Statement Below

Check whether the statement is correct or incorrect.

	Correct	Incorrect
1.		
2.		
3.		
4.		
5.		
6.		
7.		
8.		
9.		
10.		

1. There is a high incidence of injuries and deaths for motorcyclists because motorcycles provide little or no protection.

2. It is a good idea for motorists following motorcylists to maintain greater following distances during windy conditions.

3. Experienced motorcyclists often ride in the left portion of a lane, but it is actually better if they ride in the right portion of a lane.

4. Increasing your following distance between you and a large truck ahead provides additional visibility around the truck.

5. Car and truck drivers have more difficulty judging the speed and position of a motorcycle at night than during the day.

6. A helmet restricts a motorcyclist's vision and should only be worn when riding on an expressway.

7. The rear brake supplies 70 percent of a motorcycle's braking power.

8. When riding in groups, motorcyclists should always be sure to ride single file.

9. The safest and best way to learn to ride a motorcycle is to ask a friend who rides to teach you.

10. Most car-motorcycle conflicts occur on curves on rural roadways.

Name _____ Date _____

Check True or False

1. Cyclists should have their headlights on day and night as it improves their ability to be seen.

2. When driving around or near bicyclists, it is a good idea to keep extra space between your vehicle and the bicyclist.

3. Mopeds generally travel faster than motor scooters.

4. Prior to passing a bicycle or motorcycle, you should adjust your lane position to leave room.

5. Pedestrians are more vulnerable than motorcyclists.

6. Prior to leaving an alley, vehicles should stop between the sidewalk and the street, just prior to entering the street.

7. On wet roads, large trucks have shorter stopping distances than cars.

8. Vehicles are encouraged to back into any type of parking stall in a parking lot.

9. Vehicles going in all directions are required to stop whenever a school bus has stopped with its red lights on.

10. When meeting an oncoming "eighteen wheeler," you should move as far left as you can.

	True	False
1.		
2.		
3.		
4.		
5.		
6.		
7.		
8.		
9.		
10.		

Use the Picture

Study the pictures and answer the questions below.

1. What could the driver of the car have done to avoid this conflict?

_____

_____

2. What could the motorcyclist have done to avoid this situation?

_____

_____

3. What problem might this motorcyclist experience on this gravel road and why?

_____

_____

4. What following distance should this motorcyclist use on this roadway?

_____

_____

Use the Pictures

Examine the pictures below and write the mistakes made by each
motorcyclist. What action should driver X take to avoid a collision?

1. _____

   _____

   _____

   _____

2. _____

   _____

   _____

   _____

3. _____

   _____

   _____

   _____

Study the Diagram

Analyze the position of the motorcycles in relation to
vehicle X and answer the questions below.

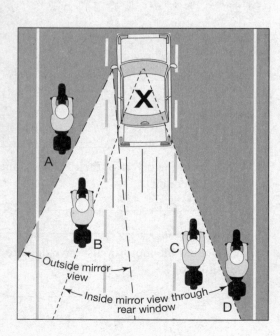

_____ 1. Which motorcyclists are in zones that cannot
be seen in either mirror?

_____ 2. Which motorcyclist is the most difficult to
see as part of the visual search pattern?

_____ 3. Which motorcyclist can be seen in the
inside mirror?

_____ 4. Which motorcyclist can be seen in the
outside mirror?

_____ 5. Which pair of motorcyclists, A and B or C
and D, is positioned correctly in their lane?

Pick a Word

Use the word or words in the box that best matches each definition below.

controlled braking	overdriving headlights
fishtailing	rocking
hydroplaning	skid

_____ 1. A tire rises up on top of water and no longer has contact with the road

_____ 2. Driving forward a little and then back a little to move your vehicle out of snow, mud, or sand

_____ 3. When tires lose all or part of their grip on the roadway while braking, accelerating, or steering

_____ 4. The rear of the vehicle swerving back and forth

_____ 5. A technique of applying your brakes to slow or stop quickly without locking your wheels

_____ 6. Driving at a speed that makes your stopping distance longer than the distance lighted by your headlights

Check Your Knowledge

Check correct or incorrect for each situation. If the statement is incorrect, write the word that makes the statement correct.

	Correct	Incorrect
1.		
2.		
3.		
4.		
5.		
6.		
7.		
8.		
9.		
10.		
11.		
12.		
13.		

Correction

1. Turn on the heater to help reduce moisture on the inside of the windshield. _____

2. The darkest days have the darkest shadows. _____

3. Move to lane position 2 if the oncoming driver does not reduce high-beam headlights. _____

4. In fog, other vehicles may be closer than you think. _____

5. Use high-beam headlights day or night when it snows. _____

6. Slushy snow in standing water can increase hydroplaning risk. _____

7. If water is just over the tire rims, drive quickly in low gear. _____

8. Apply heavy brake pressure to help dry wet brakes. _____

9. To help correct a skid, steer toward the target. _____

10. You are in a rear-wheel skid if you turn the steering wheel and the vehicle continues straight. _____

11. Correct a power-wheel skid by letting off the accelerator. _____

12. ABS will enable you to stop in a shorter distance. _____

13. When your engine gets hot, turn on your air conditioner. _____

Name _____ Date _____

Answer the Question

After you have looked at the photo and considered the low-visibility conditions, write the answers to the questions.

1. When is it safe to use high-beam headlights when other vehicles are on the road in front of you?

   _____

2. What is the most important rule for your vehicle's glass?

   _____

3. What action can you take to remind drivers to lower their high-beam headlights?

   _____

4. How can stopping distance be checked on dry pavement at night?

   _____

5. What three actions can a driver take if moisture builds up on the inside of the windshield?

   _____

   _____

   _____

Choose Your Action

Write the action you should take to reduce your risk.

Your Action

1. You encounter fog while driving.   1. _____

2. You are driving at the maximum speed limit when sleet starts to fall.   2. _____

3. It looks like the water on the road ahead will be as high as the bottom of your vehicle.   3. _____

4. You get stuck in deep snow, mud, or sand.   4. _____

5. You must drive on a heavily traveled gravel road.   5. _____

6. You need to brake hard with your ABS-equipped vehicle.   6. _____

7. Ice and slush are stuck to the underside of your vehicle when you park.   7. _____

8. You get stuck in deep snow with your engine running.   8. _____

9. Snow is packed down in the tire tracks in lane position 1.   9. _____

10. You need to check your traction in icy areas.   10. _____

Pick the Term

Use the words in the box to the right to complete the statement on traction control.

1. In a(n) _____ situation, the front wheels slide ahead instead of turning.

2. Release your accelerator if your _____ are spinning.

3. When a vehicle's rear end slides out, this is called a(n) _____.

4. In a(n) _____ situation, steer quickly and precisely.

5. The squeeze-relax-squeeze technique is used for _____ braking.

controlled
fishtail
oversteer
power wheels
understeer

Test Your Knowledge

Answer the questions below.

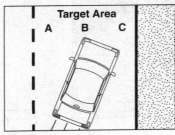

Diagram A

Diagram B

1. The vehicle in Diagram A skidded off target.

   A. Where should the driver look? Check the correct answer.

   _____ Look toward A.

   _____ Look toward B.

   _____ Look toward C.

   B. Where should the driver steer? Check the correct answer.

   _____ Steer toward A.

   _____ Steer toward B.

   _____ Steer toward C.

2. List the three steps a driver should take to control a front-wheel skid.

   _____

   _____

   _____

3. If a vehicle does not have ABS, name and describe the technique the driver should use to stop quickly.

   _____

4. In Diagram B, circle A or B for the direction the front tires would be turned when the front of the vehicle skids to the left off target.

Name _____ Date _____

Study the Picture

Study the conditions in the picture and check true or false for each statement below.

	True	False
1.		
2.		
3.		
4.		
5.		
6.		
7.		
8.		
9.		
10.		

1. Rain-covered roadways create limited traction.
2. Use cruise control on slippery roads for control.
3. Increase following distance from other vehicles.
4. Use high-beam headlights to increase visibility to others.
5. Roads are most slippery when rain starts to fall.
6. Drive in the tire tracks left by other vehicles.
7. Bald tires reduce the chance of hydroplaning.
8. A sign that the brakes are wet is the vehicle pulls to one side.
9. Estimate water depth by looking at parked vehicles.
10. If the windshield wipers must be used, turn off the headlights.

Pick a Word

Use the word or words in the box that best matches each definition below.

blowout	financial responsibility law
brake fade	grade
deductible	premium

_____ 1. Specified amount you pay to an insurance company for insurance

_____ 2. A sudden loss of air pressure in a tire

_____ 3. Loss of brake effectiveness due to overheating

_____ 4. Set amount of money you personally pay for damages that is not paid by your insurance company

_____ 5. The slope of a road surface

_____ 6. Requires you to prove that you can pay for damages you may cause with your vehicle

Test Your Knowledge

Check correct or incorrect for each situation. If the statement is incorrect, write the word or words that make the statement correct.

	Correct	Incorrect
1.		
2.		
3.		
4.		
5.		
6.		
7.		
8.		
9.		
10.		

Correction

1. If your brakes overheat, tap the brakes lightly. _____

2. Underinflation is a major cause of tire wear. _____

3. Handle a rear tire blowout like a skid. _____

4. The faster a driver travels and the shorter the distance to an obstacle, the more time the driver will have to respond. _____

5. If the engine overheats, turn on the heater. _____

6. If the headlights fail, use turn signals, parking lights, or hazard lights to see. _____

7. If there is a fire in the engine, use water to put it out. _____

8. If a front wheel leaves the roadway, use targeting and reference points to aid recovery. _____

9. If the engine stops suddenly, turn on the headlights. _____

10. If you enter a curve too fast, brake hard. _____

Choose the Action

Write the letter for the action you should execute in the emergency.

Emergency

_____ 1. Head-on collision threat

_____ 2. Large object in the roadway close
ahead

_____ 3. Flooded engine

_____ 4. Total steering failure

_____ 5. Side-impact collision threat

_____ 6. Total brake failure

_____ 7. Rear-end collision threat

_____ 8. A left-front tire blowout occurs

_____ 9. Vehicle stalled on railroad tracks,
unable to restart engine

_____ 10. Power brakes fail

Action

A. Steer firmly to the right.

B. Push the brake pedal harder.

C. Hold accelerator pedal to the floor, turn ignition
on for five seconds.

D. Use the parking brake with on-off action to slow
down.

E. Break or accelerate quickly.

F. Downshift to slow.

G. Swerve sharply.

H. Brake hard, steer right.

I. Move to an open front zone.

J. All passengers leave the vehicle.

Number the Steps

In the picture below, a collision has resulted in injury and damage.
Number the following steps in the correct order.

_____ Exchange information with others involved.

_____ Aid the injured.

_____ Pull off the roadway and stop.

_____ Send for the police.

_____ Prevent further damage.

Name _____ Date _____

Choose the Factor

Read the factors below. Check if each factor causes higher or lower insurance premiums.

1. Driver has not been convicted of any moving violations.
2. Principal driver is under 25 years of age.
3. Vehicle will be driven for a great number of miles.
4. Driver is married.
5. Driver has a "B" average or better in academic work.
6. Driver owns a sport utility vehicle.
7. Driver has frequent claims filed against the insurance company.
8. Vehicle has deductibles on collision and comprehensive coverage.

	Lower	Higher
1.		
2.		
3.		
4.		
5.		
6.		
7.		
8.		

Use the Pictures

Study the pictures, and then number the steps in the correct order for an off-road recovery.

_____ Turn the steering wheel to the right when the tire touches the roadway.

_____ Hold the steering wheel at the 9:00 and 3:00 positions.

_____ Steer toward the target.

_____ Reduce speed to 5–10 mph.

_____ Return to lane position 1.

_____ Select a safe area to return to the roadway.

_____ Turn the steering wheel slightly to the left.

Test Your Knowledge

Check true or false for each statement below.

1. Driving is still possible after the accelerator spring breaks.

2. If the hood flies up, look through the crack below the open hood.

3. At speeds over 30 mph, swerving takes more distance than braking.

4. Driving quickly through potholes reduces damage to tires.

5. If a vehicle is totally submerged under water, pressure will equalize allowing doors to be opened.

6. To minimize the effects of a collision, use changes in speed or direction to reduce the impact.

7. If a vehicle crosses over the center line into your path of travel, steer left.

8. Tires wear more quickly when drivers brake abruptly and steer sharply.

9. After a collision, you are not required to show proof of financial responsibility.

10. A compact spare tire can be used for a limited number of miles.

	True	False
1.		
2.		
3.		
4.		
5.		
6.		
7.		
8.		
9.		
10.		

Use the Diagrams

You are the driver of vehicle X in each picture below. Below each picture, write what emergency action or actions you would take.

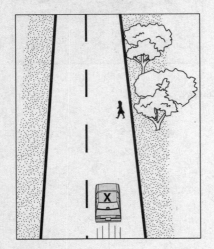

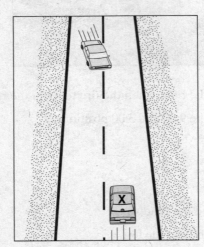

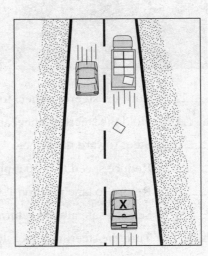

1. Action: _____
_____

2. Action: _____
_____

3. Action: _____
_____

Use the Driving in City Traffic Terms

Use the words in the box below that match each definition.

avoiding conflicts	overtake	road rage	sudden stops
blind intersection	point of no return	stale green light	tailgating
covering the brake	riding the brake		

_____ 1. Situation in which another driver is following your vehicle too closely

_____ 2. A point at which you can no longer stop safely without entering an intersection

_____ 3. A traffic light that has been green for some time and soon will turn yellow

_____ 4. Taking actions when a vehicle enters your path of travel

_____ 5. Allowing your foot to rest on the brake pedal

_____ 6. Situation in which an angry driver gets very close to your vehicle in a threatening manner

_____ 7. An intersection where your view of traffic on an intersecting road is impeded

_____ 8. Lanes next to parked vehicles may cause this problem

_____ 9. To approach and pass a slower-moving vehicle ahead of you

_____ 10. Taking your foot off the accelerator and holding it over the foot-brake pedal

Study the Diagram

The driver of vehicle X in the diagram is being tailgated. Check the box that indicates the correct or incorrect way to manage the tailgater.

1. Increase following distance to four or more seconds.

2. Turn on hazard flashers.

3. Move slightly right to give the tailgater a view ahead.

4. Signal early for turns, stops, or lane change.

5. Brake suddenly to get the tailgater's attention.

6. Flash brake lights early to warn the tailgater.

7. Accelerate to increase space between you and the tailgater.

8. Turn on left-turn signal to slow the tailgater.

9. Pull out of traffic flow to allow the tailgater to pass

10. Change speeds constantly to create space in your rear zone.

	Correct	Incorrect
1.		
2.		
3.		
4.		
5.		
6.		
7.		
8.		
9.		
10.		

Use Pictures A and B

Read each statement below about reacting to the hazards of limited space, parked vehicles, and other users shown in picture A. Check correct or incorrect for each statement.

1. Drivers should look through the windows of parked cars to identify vehicles that may be entering traffic.

2. The first clue of a possible conflict with the first parked car on the right and you is the direction of the parked vehicle's wheels.

3. At this point, it would be best to ride the brake and swerve as quickly as you can to the left.

4. If necessary, you should tap your horn to warn the driver of the parked car of your presence.

5. In this situation, you should be ready to stop or swerve at any time.

	Correct	Incorrect
1.		
2.		
3.		
4.		
5.		

Study picture B and list the four advantages of maintaining a 3-second (or more) following distance.

1. _____

2. _____

3. _____

4. _____

Mark the Best Lane Choice

You are driving on a wide city street with three lanes in each direction. Check the best lane to drive for each situation below.

1. You intend to turn left at the next intersection.

2. The lane that offers the most constant speed on a three-lane roadway.

3. You are driving slowly while a friend looks for a street number on the right.

4. You hear and see an emergency vehicle approaching and prepare to stop.

5. You need to pass a vehicle that is traveling slowly in the center lane.

6. You intend to turn right at the next intersection.

7. The best overall lane for traveling all the way through a town.

	Left Lane	Center Lane	Right Lane
1.			
2.			
3.			
4.			
5.			
6.			
7.			

Encountering City Traffic

The statements below describe actions you may take when you encounter various situations in city traffic. Check true or false for each statement.

	True	False
1.		
2.		
3.		
4.		
5.		

1. It is illegal to pass another vehicle at an intersection.

2. Due to slower speeds, there are fewer driving hazards in city driving areas than in rural driving areas.

3. In order to gain time to think and respond in city areas, you must reduce your speed.

4. You should always try to use a half-block visual lead when driving in a city area.

5. When being tailgated, you should use a 4-second (or more) space margin to the front.

Adjusting to City Traffic Problems

Answer each of the following questions using the space provided.

1. In addition to adjusting your speed ahead of time for other drivers that may block your way, and driving with traffic flow, what other guide should be used in selecting the best speed in city areas?

   _____

2. When driving along parked vehicles, how far away should you be from any parked vehicle?

   _____

3. Why are one-way streets usually safer to drive on than 2-way streets?

   _____

4. What actions would you take and how would you warn an oncoming driver that he or she is traveling the wrong way on a one-way street?

   _____

5. You know that the 3-second rule is not your total stopping distance, but what does this rule protect you from?

   _____

Searching for City Traffic Problems

List three ways to identify a one-way street.

1. _____

2. _____

   _____

3. _____

List three high-risk areas for sudden stops.

1. _____

2. _____

3. _____

Identify Safe Following Guidelines

Check yes or no to tell if using the 3-second following rule is a safe procedure in each situation below.

1. You are pulling a heavy load or a recreational vehicle.
2. You have good traction and you are an alert driver.
3. You are being tailgated.
4. You are a beginning driver.
5. The driver ahead of you seems to be driving erratically.

	Yes	No
1.		
2.		
3.		
4.		
5.		

Use the Picture

The picture shows many different traffic situations. Use the picture to answer the questions provided.

1. On which street must the vehicles yield the right of way?

   _____

2. What lane should driver F change to before turning left?

   _____

3. What lane should driver F turn into?

   _____

4. Why are lanes A and C high-risk areas for sudden stops?

   _____

5. What hazards to the right should driver M identify?

   _____

6. What action should driver M take?

   _____

7. What error is driver L making?

   _____

8. Which lane (A, B, or C) is the safest lane for through traffic?

   _____

9. Which vehicle is in car M's rear-zone blind spot?

   _____

10. Can driver J turn right?

    _____

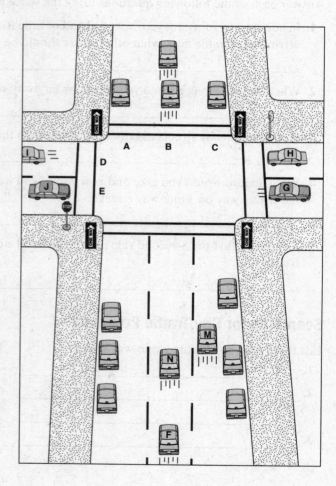

Pick a Word

Use the words in the box below that match each definition.

advisory speed sign	pull-out area
flash flood	roadway shoulder
line of sight	runaway vehicle ramp
median	slow-moving vehicle
multilane roadway	switchback

_____ 1. Rural roads with more than one lane going in the same direction

_____ 2. A vehicle usually identified by an orange triangular sign at the rear

_____ 3. Gives suggested travel speed for curve under ideal conditions

_____ 4. An additional right lane for slower-moving vehicles

_____ 5. A grass, metal, or concrete divider that separates traffic moving in opposite directions

_____ 6. The distance you can see ahead in the direction you are looking when driving

_____ 7. Sudden rush of water due to excessive rain

_____ 8. Series of sharp turns, often found in mountain areas

_____ 9. A paved, gravel, or soft area to the left or right of the roadway

_____ 10. An area specially designed to slow a vehicle that loses the ability to brake when going down a steep hill

Test Your Knowledge

Check correct or incorrect for each statement below.

	Correct	Incorrect
1.		
2.		
3.		
4.		
5.		
6.		
7.		
8.		
9.		
10.		

1. There are more fatalities in rural driving than in city driving mainly due to the number of hills and curves.

2. When crossing multilane highways, you should treat each side as a one-way street.

3. Lower gears might provide more power while going up steep hills.

4. It is illegal for you to speed up while being passed by another vehicle.

5. The 3-second following distance is the safest space cushion for all types of conditions in rural driving.

6. As you approach a hill in your vehicle, your line of sight becomes shorter.

7. When driving downhill, you should maintain steady pressure on the brake.

8. Move to lane position 1 when you cannot see oncoming vehicles on mountain curves.

9. If caught in a sandstorm and you must drive, use your low-beam headlights.

10. On a divided highway, all vehicles must stop for a loading school bus.

Name _____ Date _____

Study the Diagram

While traveling on a two-lane highway, another vehicle decides to pass vehicle A. The pass is safe and legal. Vehicle A is moving at a speed 15 miles under the limit. Starting with position 1, match the letter of each step of the passing maneuver below with the correct vehicle position number.

	Vehicle Position
1.	
2.	
3.	
4.	
5.	
6.	
7.	
8.	
9.	
10.	

A. Check for canceled left signal.

B. Change lanes smoothly.

C. Check rearview mirror for the headlights of vehicle A.

D. Check for canceled right signal; adjust speed.

E. Accelerate to proper speed.

F. Pass vehicle A.

G. Tap horn or flash headlights.

H. Return to right lane.

I. Check rear zones through mirror and mirror blind spot; signal right.

J. Check mirror blind spot; signal left

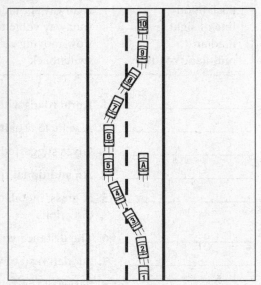

Identify the Area to Scan

You are driving on the rural highway shown in the picture. Check which visual search area you would scan to identify each of the following.

1. Traffic controls

2. Side road on the right

3. Your speed

4. A car too close in the rear zone

5. Potholes in the roadway

6. Your fuel supply

7. A car in the left-rear zone

8. Oncoming traffic

9. Your headlights on high or low beams

10. Directional changes in the roadway

	Ahead	Sides	Mirrors	Instrument Panel
1.				
2.				
3.				
4.				
5.				
6.				
7.				
8.				
9.				
10.				

Name _____ Date _____

List the Potential Conflicts

Study the picture provided. You are the driver of the vehicle behind
the truck. Answer the questions to the right.

1. List four potential problems that may change
   your path of travel.

   a. _____

   b. _____

   c. _____

   d. _____

2. What actions might you need to take?

   a. _____

   b. _____

3. What would you do if a vehicle from behind
   began to pass you?

   a. _____

   b. _____

4. What potential problem might the roadway
   cause in your path of travel?

   a. _____

5. Should any of the vehicles shown prepare to
   pass in this situation?

   a. _____

Write Your Decision

Write the missing word or words that complete each statement on the blanks.

1. _____   1. Prior to passing, drivers should make sure they can answer yes or no to whether
                          it is legal, if it is _____, and if it is safe.

2. _____   2. Passing is normally not allowed when within 100 feet of a two-lane bridge, a(n)
                          _____, or an underpass.

3. _____   3. After driving through a severe sandstorm, drivers should change the oil, oil filter,
                          and _____.

4. _____   4. Shift to a _____ gear before starting to drive downhill on a mountain
                          roadway.

Write the Parts of the Procedure

List five parts of the procedure for safely driving around a curve.

1. _____

2. _____

3. _____

4. _____

5. _____

Use the Pictures

In each picture below, you are driving vehicle X at 50 mph on a two-lane highway with no oncoming or following traffic. Below each picture, circle the action to take and tell why on the blank lines.

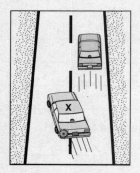  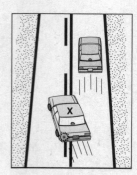 

Pass   Follow   Pass   Follow   Pass   Follow   Pass   Follow

1. Why? _____   **2. Why?** _____   **3. Why?** _____   **4. Why?** _____

_____   _____   _____   _____

_____   _____   _____   _____

Determine Driver Actions

The diagram to the right shows a divided multilane highway. The highway has a crossover area for traffic from the east to enter in order for them to travel south.

Vehicle B wants to cross over then turn left.

Vehicles A and D are both traveling northbound.

Vehicles E and F are traveling southbound.

Vehicle C is a tractor-semitrailer that is stalled on the roadway.

Study the diagram. Determine which action (listed below) each vehicle's driver should take. Write the letter of the vehicle on the blank next to each action.

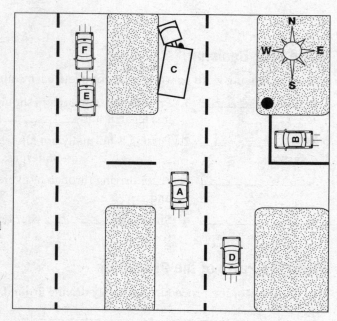

_____ **1.** Lane change as soon as possible.

_____ **2.** Remain stopped until all northbound traffic clears.

_____ **3.** Establish a 3-second following position.

_____ **4.** Be prepared to make a quick stop.

_____ **5.** Engage the hazard flashers.

Name _____ Date _____

Pick a Word

Use the word or words in the box that best matches each definition below.

acceleration lane	deceleration lane	highway hypnosis	merging area
common speed	entrance ramp	hole in traffic	velocitation
controlled-access highway	exit ramp		

_____ 1. Speed used by most drivers who drive on an expressway

_____ 2. Condition in which a driver unconsciously drives too fast after leaving an expressway

_____ 3. Allows the driver to search for a gap while picking up speed to match traffic flow

_____ 4. Type of expressway where vehicles can enter or leave only at an interchange

_____ 5. An added lane in which to slow your vehicle without slowing vehicles to the rear on the expressway

_____ 6. Condition in which a driver is lulled into an inattentive, drowsy state

_____ 7. Leads off of the expressway and allows the driver to look for a speed change and slow the vehicle

_____ 8. Allows the driver to evaluate path of travel, control zones, and determine the best entry speed

_____ 9. Allows the driver to evaluate time and space prior to moving into traffic flow

_____ 10. Empty space between traffic clusters

Use the Diagram

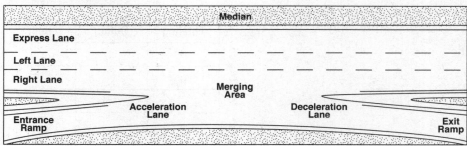

Study the diagram above. Write the expressway term that matches each definition below.

1. Ramp that gives you access to an expressway _____

2. Area that separates two-way traffic on an expressway _____

3. Ramp that leads a vehicle off an expressway _____

4. Added lane on an expressway in which to slow a vehicle without blocking vehicles behind _____

5. Part of an expressway entrance you enter at the same speed as vehicles in the nearest lane _____

6. Part of an expressway entrance that allows you to increase speed to that of vehicles on the expressway _____

7. Expressway lane with few exits, used by traffic during morning and evening rush hours _____

Test Your Knowledge

Check correct or incorrect for each statement below about
expressways.

	Correct	Incorrect
1.		
2.		
3.		
4.		
5.		

1. Cross traffic is eliminated on controlled-access expressways because
   there are no intersections.

2. Expressways have a median strip or barrier between opposing lanes
   of traffic.

3. Expressways have narrow shoulders and underpasses.

4. Pedestrians, nonmotorized vehicles, and slow-moving vehicles are
   permitted on most expressways.

5. Expressways are designed to help drivers anticipate conditions
   ahead.

List Expressway Strategies

List four strategies to use to become a safe highway driver.

1. _____

2. _____

3. _____

4. _____

Identify Problem Areas

Check the box to the right that identifies different problems you
must look for when entering and exiting expressways.

	Entering	Exiting	Both
1.			
2.			
3.			
4.			
5.			
6.			
7.			
8.			
9.			
10.			
11.			

1. Crossing paths with traffic
2. Roadway repair activity
3. Ramp signal light
4. High wall blocks vision
5. Ramp overflow
6. Merging area
7. Short acceleration lane
8. Wrong ramp choice
9. Short deceleration lane
10. Gap difficult to find
11. WRONG WAY or DO NOT ENTER sign

Name _____ Date _____

Check the Lane

Above is a group of signs over an expressway. Check the correct lane for each question below.

	Far Left Lane	Left Center Lane	Center Lane	Right Center Lane	Far Right Lane
1.					
2.					
3.					
4.					
5.					

1. Which lane should you use to go to Springfield?

2. Which lane should you use to go to Columbus?

3. Which lane should you use to exit highway 56?

4. Which two lanes can you use to go to Miami?

5. Which two lanes of the expressway are ending?

Use the Diagram

Study the diagram. Write what actions to take at each of the five numbered points.

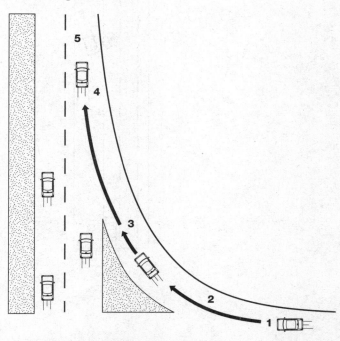

1. a. _____

   b. _____

2. a. _____

   b. _____

   c. _____

3. a. _____

   b. _____

   c. _____

4. a. _____

5. a. _____

   b. _____

   c. _____

Name _____ Date _____

Use the Picture

You are driving car X on an expressway with a view of traffic ahead as shown in the picture below. Check yes or no for each statement.

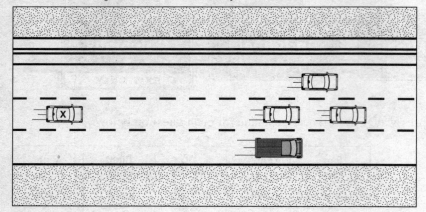

1. A wolf pack is forming ahead.

2. You should accelerate to join the cars ahead.

3. Maintain speed; be a "loner."

4. A driver in a wolf pack is likely to have trouble with lane changes.

5. If you are tailgated, speed up so the wolf pack protects you.

	Yes	No
1.		
2.		
3.		
4.		
5.		

Match the Location

Study the picture of the expressway exits. Write the letter of the location that matches where each action should take place.

_____ **1.** Give right turn signal to use exit S.

_____ **2.** Begin to decelerate for exit S.

_____ **3.** Change to deceleration lane for exit N.

_____ **4.** Adjust to exit ramp speed for exit N.

_____ **5.** Give right turn signal to use exit N.

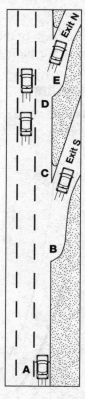

Pick a Word

Use the words in the box to complete each statement below.

alternative fuel	electronic control module
budget	muffler
catalytic converter	Variable Ride-Height Suspension

1. _____ come from resources other than petroleum and are reducing our dependence on imported oil.   _____

2. All modern vehicles have a computer or _____ located in the engine compartment that controls your engine's efficiency.   _____

3. _____ are used in the exhaust system to reduce the levels of nitrogen oxides, which the sun heats into smog.   _____

4. When considering your _____, you must understand the real cost of owning a vehicle.   _____

5. The _____ raises or lowers the ride height of the vehicle while it is in motion.   _____

6. The _____ reduces the noise from combustion sounds in the engine.   _____

Costs of Owning a Vehicle

List some of the *major* expenses of owning a vehicle.

1. _____
2. _____
3. _____
4. _____
5. _____

List some of the operating costs of owning a vehicle.

6. _____
7. _____
8. _____
9. _____
10. _____

Correct or Incorrect

Read the statements below and check whether the statement is correct or incorrect.

	Correct	Incorrect
1.		
2.		
3.		
4.		
5.		
6.		
7.		
8.		
9.		
10.		

1. Changing the oil is the key to keeping your vehicle in good running condition.

2. Carburetors are replacing fuel injection systems in newer cars because they increase performance and decrease fuel consumption.

3. A battery contains a strong acid that can cause severe injury.

4. Windshield wiper fluid is an appropriate substitution for coolant.

5. Static electricity can spark a fire or explosion.

6. Leaking purple fluid is an indication of a broken transmission seal.

7. There are two types of brakes: disk brakes on the front wheels, and snare brakes on the rear wheels.

8. Periodically check tire pressure when tires are warm.

9. When a wear bar is visible, replace the tire.

10. A tire with a traction grade of C has better traction performance than a tire with a grade of B.

Test Your Knowledge

Complete each of the following statements.

1. You should avoid touching battery fluid because it _____ that can burn your skin.

2. You should _____ the tires regularly to promote even wear.

3. _____ pressure causes tires to wear quickly and can cause tire failure.

4. Many cars use fuel most efficiently at a speed of _____.

Name _____ Date _____

Use the Picture

Use the picture on the right to list the four
steps (by letter) for connecting jumper cables.

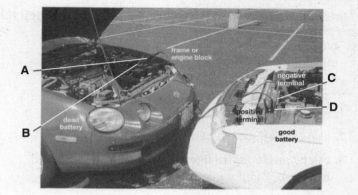

_____ **1.** First connection

_____ **2.** Second connection

_____ **3.** Third connection

_____ **4.** Fourth connection

Test Your Knowledge

Check the box to the right that best applies to each statement below.

1. Probably best selection of high-quality used vehicles due to trade-ins on new vehicles

2. Usually less expensive to insure

3. Experience quick depreciation

4. Largest variety of used vehicles

5. Dealer might not have repair facilities

6. Price probably will be highest of all

7. A warranty is usually offered

8. Usually gives lowest price

9. Dealer seldom provides a warranty

10. Also offers a lease along with a buy option

	Used-Car Dealer	New-Car Dealer
1.		
2.		
3.		
4.		
5.		
6.		
7.		
8.		
9.		
10.		

Study the Diagram

Identify the part of the tire that matches each statement.

_____ **1.** Federal laws require tire manufacturers to place standardized information here.

_____ **2.** The higher the grade (60–500), the longer this should last.

_____ **3.** Ratings are based on the tire's ability to stop on wet concrete or asphalt. The higher the grade (AA to C) the better.

_____ **4.** Tires become unsafe when this is down to 1/16 of an inch and the wear bars are seen.

_____ **5.** Ratings A–C (A is highest) are an indication of a tire's resistance to heat.

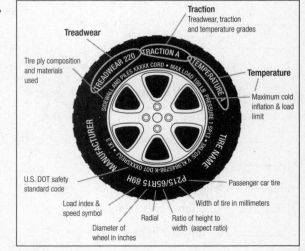

Alternative Fuels

Match the description to the type of alternative fuel that it best describes.

biodiesel	natural gas
ethanol	propane
hydrogen	

1. produced domestically from corn and other crops _____

2. also called liquefied petroleum gas _____

3. can be produced from fossil fuels. Vehicles powered by this fuel emit **no** harmful air pollutants. _____

4. derived from vegetable oils and animal fats _____

5. is a fossil fuel that generates less air pollutants _____

Use the Picture

Study the illustration. Use your textbook to select the letter that identifies the parts of a car alarm.

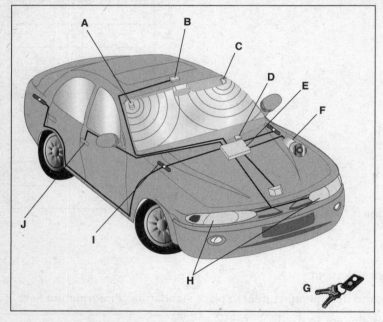

_____ **1.** interior pressure sensor

_____ **2.** alarm brain

_____ **3.** keycode receiver

_____ **4.** shock sensor

_____ **5.** crossover unit

_____ **6.** door sensor

_____ **7.** alarm speaker

_____ **8.** lights

_____ **9.** microphone sensor

_____ **10.** interior light

Pick a Word

Use the word or words in the box that matches each definition below.

Global Positioning System (GPS)   recreational vehicle index   safety chains legend

_____ 1. Camper or self-contained motor home primarily used for vacation

_____ 2. A network of satellites used for mapping and navigating

_____ 3. A chart that explains markings and symbols used on a map

_____ 4. Shows a listing of cities and roads

_____ 5. Keeps a trailer from breaking loose from a vehicle if the trailer becomes unhitched

Test Your Knowledge

Check true or false for each statement below.

	True	False
1.		
2.		
3.		
4.		
5.		
6.		
7.		
8.		
9.		
10.		
11.		
12.		

1. Always carry a spare can of fuel when traveling on a long-distance trip.

2. In order to stay alert on a long-distance trip, take a break every two hours.

3. Your front view is reduced when driving a recreational vehicle.

4. The safest way to back a recreational vehicle is to sound the horn and check the outside mirrors often.

5. Use the 4-second following rule when driving a recreational vehicle.

6. Drivers often fail to observe reduced height and width signs when driving large vehicles such as motor homes.

7. Recreational vehicles hold the roadway better in windy conditions because of their size and weight.

8. Pulling a trailer increases a vehicle's fuel economy because of the tire's increased pressure.

9. When loading a trailer, put about 10 percent of the total weight on the hitch of the trailer.

10. If a trailer starts to fishtail, apply the brakes hard and steer toward the shoulder of the roadway.

11. When towing a trailer, allow twice as much distance to pass.

12. On a long-distance trip, the safest maximum distance to drive each day is 400 miles.

Use Trip Planning Skills

Read the following story. Choose an action from the list to the right for each situation presented below. You will use some action responses more than once.

You are staying with a friend in an unfamiliar area. You must arrive for a job interview early in the morning at an office ten miles away from your friend's house.

_____ 1. Your friend tells you that the area has an hour-long rush hour.

_____ 2. The weather forecast is for a temperature of 10 degrees below zero.

_____ 3. The weather forecast is for a warm, sunny, and clear day.

_____ 4. The weather forecast is for foggy weather with poor visibility.

_____ 5. The traffic report says there will be heavy traffic as usual, but no delays.

_____ 6. The traffic report says that a roadway you will use is blocked by three separate collisions.

_____ 7. While making a routine check, you find your tire pressure is low.

_____ 8. You forgot to get fuel the night before, and you are almost on "empty" and need to fill up.

_____ 9. The route you have selected to get to the interview has many uncontrolled intersections.

_____ 10. You miss the street on which the company you are visiting is located.

A.	Allow more travel time.
B.	Drive slowly for the first few miles to warm up the car.
C.	Proceed as planned.
D.	Choose another route.
E.	Check tire pressure; add air.
F.	Allow time to stop for fuel.
G.	Drive around the block.

Using Skills

Complete the sentences by writing in the missing words below.

_____ 1. Have your car serviced at least _____ before a long-distance trip.

_____ 2. Inflate tires to the _____ recommended pressure before carrying heavy loads in your car.

_____ 3. On a long trip, eat _____ food than usual.

_____ 4. To save fuel, combine several _____.

_____ 5. Today trip planning can be done by surfing the _____.

Name _____ Date _____

Use the Map

Using the map to answer the questions below, calculate traveling times and distances.

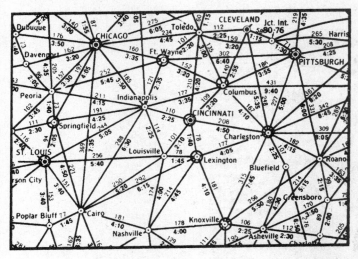

_____ **1.** How many miles is Springfield, IL, from St. Louis, MO?

_____ **2.** How much estimated time will it take to travel from Lexington, KY, to Knoxville, TN, traveling at 55 mph?

_____ **3.** Which route is shorter going from Columbus, OH, to Knoxville, TN?
  A. By way of Cincinnati, OH
  B. By way of Charleston, WV

_____ **4.** How far is it from Chicago, IL, to Pittsburgh, PA, by way of Ft. Wayne, IN?

_____ **5.** How much estimated time would it take to travel the distance for the trip described in item 4?

Use the Chart

Using the mileage chart on the right, answer the questions below.

_____ **1.** How far is it from Albuquerque, NM, to Boston, MA?

_____ **2.** What is the distance from Chicago, IL, to Billings, MT?

_____ **3.** How far is it from Columbia, SC, to Baltimore, MD?

_____ **4.** What is the distance from Charleston, SC, to Albany, NY?

_____ **5.** Your car gets 25 miles to the gallon. How many gallons of fuel do you need to drive from Boise, ID, to Atlanta, GA?

	Albany, NY	Albuquerque, NM	Atlanta, GA	Baltimore, MD	Billings, MT
Albany, NY		2041	1010	339	2098
Albuquerque, NM	2041		1404	1890	991
Atlanta, GA	1010	1404		654	1799
Billings, MT	2098	991	1799	1916	
Birmingham, AL	1071	1254	150	771	1775
Boise, ID	2518	940	2223	2406	606
Boston, MA	169	2220	1108	427	2197
Buffalo, NY	301	1773	907	366	1755
Calgary, AB	2434	1544	2369	2309	663
Charleston, SC	880	1703	291	568	2175
Charleston, WV	636	1600	501	362	1721
Charlotte, NC	169	2220	1108	427	2197
Chicago, IL	301	1773	907	366	1755
Cleveland, OH	2434	1544	2369	2309	663
Columbia, SC	880	1703	291	568	2175

Name _____ Date _____

Use the Map

Use the map shown to answer the questions below. Items 1–5 focus on location by using letters and numbers along the edge of the map. Items 6–10 focus on identifying highways by using the map legend.

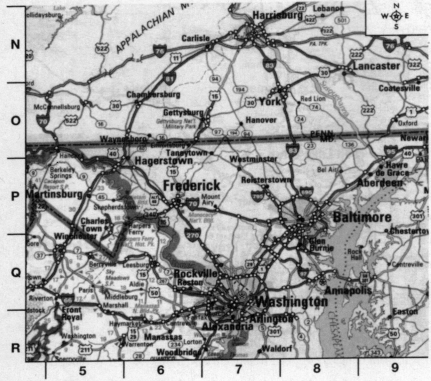

Map © by Rand McNally R.L. #98-S-135

_____ 1. What letter and number shows the location of Carlisle?

_____ 2. What town is on U.S. 222 in the location of *N-8*?

_____ 3. Traveling northeast on Interstate 95 out of Baltimore, what is the first city you would pass in location *P-9*?

_____ 4. What letter and number shows the location of Easton?

_____ 5. What letter and number gives the location of Reisterstown?

_____ 6. Near what interstate highway is Frederick?

_____ 7. What interstate highway would you use to go from Rockville northwest to Hagerstown?

_____ 8. What U.S. highway would you use to get from York to Lancaster?

_____ 9. What two routes could you use to get from Havre de Grace to Baltimore?

_____ 10. What state highway would you travel to go from Carlisle to Reisterstown?